Students, Structures, Spaces

Activities in the Built Environment

Aase Eriksen

Marjorie Wintermute

Addison-Wesley Publishing Company
Menlo Park, California • Reading, Massachusetts
London • Amsterdam • Don Mills, Ontario • Sydney

Excerpts from How Much Room Do You Need (page 103) and Where Do the Bubbles Go? (page 110) adapted from *The Hidden Dimension* by Edward T. Hall. Copyright © 1966 by Edward T. Hall. Reprinted by permission of Doubleday & Company, Inc.

This book is published by the ADDISON-WESLEY INNOVATIVE DIVISION.

Design: Ellen Schmutz and Tom Emerson
Production Design: Michelle Taverniti
Drawings by Alan Ward

ISBN-0-201-10486-5
ABCDEFGH-ML-898765432

INTRODUCTION

The built environment is architecture in its broadest sense—the cities, streets, houses, schools, parks, skyscrapers, bridges, and barns that we build and the spaces that connect them. It frames our actions and in many ways determines the shape of our lives. It provides the settings in which we most often walk, sleep, eat, travel, work, or play.

Until recently, in the context of environmental studies, the built environment has been considered only as it impinges upon and destroys the natural environment. But clearly the built environment should be seen in a more positive light, for all of us spend most of our lives in a constructed setting rather than in a truly natural one. We should become more aware of how the built environment affects us, both positively and negatively, as space that people have shaped to human dimensions in such a way that it will respond to human needs, both practical and aesthetic.

Because of the roles played by the built environment in our lives, all of us from children through the elderly can benefit from learning more about it. And whether that education be self-directed, as the child learns to cope with obstacles such as stairs, or takes place in the more formal setting of the classroom, built environment education is an important, even vital process. It is important, first, for the sake of the built environment itself, and for us. Our efforts to create more livable settings around us depend on our awareness and appreciation of the importance of the built environment. Second, the built environment can provide a concreteness to the learning process—it gives us rooms to measure, spaces to study for mathematical concepts, buildings for the understanding of history, neighborhoods and towns for civic studies—that is, the built environment provides a learning laboratory for any academic study. Built environment education is not a new subject to be added to an already full curriculum. Rather, it is an approach to traditional areas of study and can be integrated with ease into existing curriculum.

The goals of built environment education are several: in schools or the community, it should stress the development, first, of an *awareness* of surroundings, senses, feelings, and needs; then, of an *understanding* of the functions and the impact of the environment; and finally, of the ability to use the environment well and to take *action*, to change it to better satisfy the needs that have been defined. The long-range objective is, of course, to make better future citizens, capable of making informed environmental decisions to improve the community. STU-

DENTS, STRUCTURES, SPACES: *Activities in the Built Environment* is a vehicle for teachers to use in working toward achieving these goals and objectives.

The Importance of the Built Environment

The built environment affects us every moment, even though that effect is often unconscious. The setting may direct our actions, as we follow a path or a hallway, or it may prevent them, when we come to a wall or must knock on a door. The setting may create or oppress our attitudes and moods, whether we are exhilarated by the beauty of a fountain in a park or feel confined by a horizon which stops abruptly at the housetops across the street.

Indeed, our entire lives are given as much to interacting and coping with the built environment as they are given to other human beings. As infants and children we explore a limited environment that gradually enlarges from the space of the crib to the entire house, the route to school, and the classroom. As we grow older, our mobility increases and our world expands, from our neighborhood, town, or city to foreign places experienced in travel. With age, our environment often narrows again, limited to our town, community center, or senior citizens housing. That a sense of place is extremely important to us is indicated by the intense memories of pleasant and unpleasant spaces that linger throughout our lives.

To develop an awareness of surroundings, children need to develop their senses, to learn what space, structure, shape, form, scale, light and shadow, texture, and color mean, and to acquire a consciousness of themselves within the surroundings. Children can then evaluate the environment in terms of human responses and become aware of how the environment feels, how it influences actions and emotions, and how various aspects of it serve or hinder human needs. Because the built environment is immediately available, it can become the laboratory in which children learn these things: the form of a building's facade, the effect of light and shadow in a hall, the texture of the walls or furnishings in a room are all at hand for the teacher to use.

Sensory awareness must be accompanied by understanding. Children must begin to think about the functions of the built environment, how it works, and how it influences attitudes and activities. As their understanding grows, they will begin to use the environment to its fullest and to make the most of the opportunities it offers.

Once children have become sensorily aware and understanding users of their surroundings, they are able to participate in improving the built environment. They begin to think about what they like and dislike and about how feelings and value judgments may be translated into changes. They learn to think creatively, to become inventors and designers of their surroundings rather than passive onlookers, to remake and use wisely their own world.

Thus, education for both children and adults about the built environment is as important as increased awareness of the natural environment. But there is no Sierra Club for our towns and cities. Concern over built environment education has developed and increased in the last ten years but has been largely scattered among local community institutions and professional groups. Only recently have larger scale efforts been made to extend built environment education throughout the nation.

The Architects-in-Schools Program

Perhaps the most extensive program for built environment education has been the Architects-in-Schools program of the National Endowment for the Arts. Since 1976, AIS has put over 250 architects and designers in schools in 45 states reaching over 500,000 students. These architects help place built environment education within the context of the school curriculum as a framework for learning in all areas. Collaborating with teachers and students, the architects contribute their own awareness of space and structure, their ability to analyze the surroundings, and their familiarity with the process and tools of design. The architect is a resource, a professional who can communicate the tools, skills, and concepts of his or her discipline to the community at large, beginning with its young people.

Some of the methods of built environment education are field trips, walks, and tours, model building, mapping, drawing, writing, lectures, and presentations. In essence, the students, teachers, and architects go through the design process together, studying the built environment, analyzing its success or failure to meet the users' needs, and effecting changes in the environment when necessary or desired. The visible results of the AIS residencies have included remodeled classrooms and libraries, renovated playgrounds, hallway murals, landscaping, neighborhood historical surveys, and solar greenhouses. The less visible results have included students and teachers with a new sense of concern for and control over their immediate surroundings, an exitement over new possibilities in learning, and a renewed interest in school spurred by hands-on activities in and out of the school building.

The real measure of the program's success is in the accomplishments of the children. For example, a math teacher in upstate New York involved her students in measuring and constructing a model of their room with the primary aim of using that process as a vehicle for teaching math. These fourth and fifth graders were at least two years behind their classmates in basic math skills. They had trouble with multiplication and division; they could not read the marking on a ruler, nor could they understand the concept of fractions. The architect assisted the teacher in making these abstractions real for the students.

Standardized test scores gained from pre-and post-testing showed that most of these students advanced one to two full grade levels in measurement and fractions. And they did equally well in multiplication, problem-solving, and abstract reasoning. In addition, their finished product—the classroom model—was most impressive, the envy of all in the school. According to their teacher, this was the first time the children in remedial math thought of themselves as "special" in a positive sense; they gained pride and self-esteem through the experience.

This is not an isolated success story. Across the country architects working with teachers have had remarkable results through built-environment education, not only at all age levels, but at all levels of ability—from gifted to learning disabled to mentally retarded. Kindergarteners in New York created an enclosed private space by building only two walls; a drafting class in Utah went through a step-by-step process of analyzing their needs and then redesigned their room to satisfy those needs; in Oklahoma an outdoor classroom was constructed.

There are hundreds of such success stories in the AIS program, and the activities in this book can provide equal success for any teacher. No special training is needed, for these activities have been used by teachers without the aid of an architect. These activities will provide concrete, hands-on experiences for the students, allowing them to learn from the built environment directly. Built environment education is a point of view that provides a framework for any subject matter and a basis for interdisciplinary studies. Built environment education is a way to connect the learning of mathematics, social studies, art, language, indeed all fields of study.

How to Use This Book

The activities in this book can be used either as a unit or individually. They are placed sequentially in each section, but can also stand by themselves. It might be wise to first read through the activities quickly to get a sense of the content of built environment education and also to see how this content can serve as a framework for enriching the existing curriculum. Each activity is presented with related subject matter—thus, for example, a third grade teacher looking for math-related materials will find an abundance of suggestions for activities. These activities have been used for all levels of students in all educational environments, and can easily be adjusted to suit the appropriate level of development.

The final section, Useful Tools and Techniques (page 179), gives suggestions that are applicable thoughout the book. You may want to introduce these activities at the beginning of the year, so that students will be familiar with the methods discussed. Note that beginning on page 192 there is a vocabulary list, in which the new terms introduced in the book are defined.

All the activities have been tested in the field by the authors and by teachers and architects in the Architects-in-Schools program, which Aase Eriksen designed and directed. The final testing of the activities was done by Marjorie Wintermute in classrooms in the Washington County, Oregon, Education Service District.

We want to thank the staff of Educational Futures, Inc., which has been part of the evaluation of these activities, and especially John Carstens for final support in editing and typing.

CONTENTS

1 TUNING INTO THE ENVIRONMENT

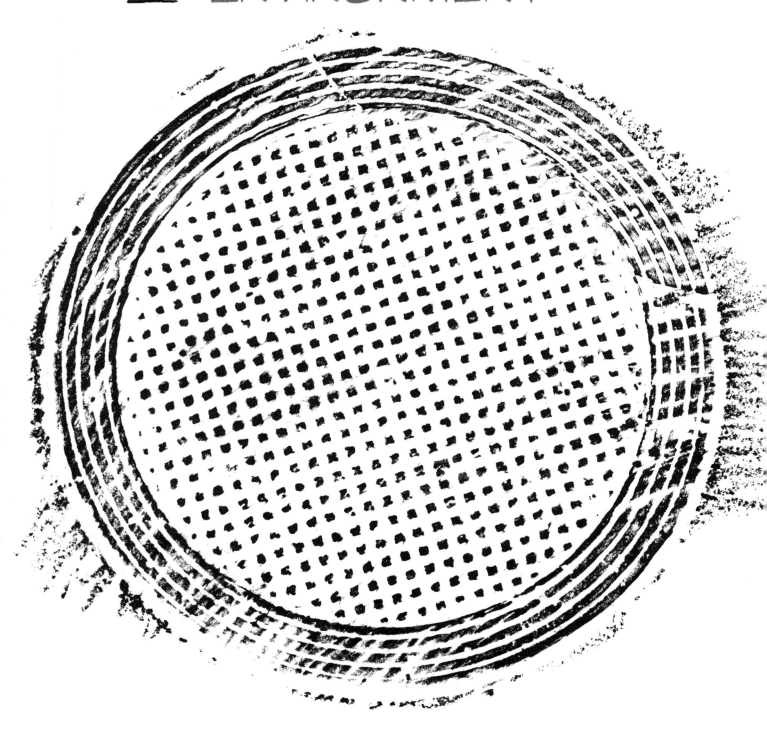

INTRODUCTION

Theme

With the accelerated pace of today's living, the constant impact of the media, and the physical growth around us, so many sensory messages are trying to get through to us that often we just turn off. This can lead to lack of concern for what happens to the environment. Sensitivity to the surrounding world requires expanding our ability to see and to put perceptions in some orderly form so they can be remembered, communicated, and acted upon.

The Activities

1. Do You See What You Think You See?
2. How Do You Feel About Your Environment?
3. Pictures in Your Mind
4. Putting It on the Dotted Line
5. Playing a Building
6. What Do You See Here?

These activities will help students understand that they don't always see the really important things in their environment and that they can expand their ability to look and see.

Curriculum Areas

Social Studies through becoming more familiar with the environment, understanding individual differences in perceptions, and developing concern for environmental decisions

Math through working with relative scales, counting, and checklists

Science through increased sensory awareness and understanding of spatial relationships

Language Arts through new vocabulary and relating words and images

Art and Music through the relationship of such concepts as balance, rhythm, symmetry, repetition, and order

Where

In the classroom

Why

So much of what is seen comes from passive experience that requires no involvement. It becomes easy to be only a spectator. Neither response nor action is necessary until something happens that has the potential to create a crisis. More could be accomplished by planning before a problem reaches crisis proportions. This requires citizens who are able to perceive, to visualize, and to anticipate. These activities offer some ways of developing these qualities through training of perceptual and observational abilities and through creative thinking.

Extensions

Using the word format (page 8) for evaluating a place in several different types of environments provides the opportunity for comparisons. Use it as a spelling lesson.

Make the fantasy trip a daily or weekly activity creating a different "picture in the mind" each time.

Have students develop dot pictures to try out on other students in the class.

Make the music and picture activity a weekly experience.

Draw floor plans of the classroom, the supermarket, or some other neighborhood place.

Bibliography

Experiencing Architecture by Steen E. Rasmussen, MIT Press, Cambridge, Mass., 1962.

This classic work deals with awareness of the built environment through the various human senses, helping us not only to see a building, but to experience and thereby understand it.

Put Your Mother on the Ceiling (Mind Pictures) by Robert Demille, Viking Penguin, New York, 1976.

A small paperback that includes a series of mind trips (fantasies), presented progressively, which could be used on a daily or weekly basis.

DO YOU SEE WHAT YOU THINK YOU SEE?

Theme

Because of conditioning or superficial observation, often what we see is only what we expect to see. If the environment is seen in this way, the most important things may be missed. The two visual imaging tricks in this activity can be used to make this point. They provide an introduction to the concept of the need to tune in to the environment.

Learning Objectives

To increase visual perception and observation

Subject Matter

Social Studies
Language Arts

Time

One-half hour

Vocabulary Words

image

Materials

Copies for each student of the sheet, "Do You See What You Think You See?"

Procedure

We are going to have a little fun testing your ability to see **images.** Some of you may see the image immediately, so play along a little. Don't give it away until the others have had a chance to figure it out.

Hold a copy of the sheet, "Do You See What You Think You See?" up in front of the class. Slowly turn the word BEE (symbolizing Built Environment Education) around. Turn it sideways, upside down, and to the opposite side before turning it right side up. While you are doing this ask . . .

What shapes do you see? (Possibilities they may come up with are squares, a hat, electric plugs, trees.)

After you have turned it around a couple of times, stop at the right side up position and ask . . .

Do you see a BEE in this image?

Slowly ask . . .

Are you looking for an insect? Or the letter *b*? Or do you see the word *BEE*?

You will begin to see the students' faces change as they see the word.

You can almost feel your mind click over as you change your focus from the black images to the white.

Some still may not see the word until you place a strip of dark paper along the top and one along the bottom.

It is easier to focus on the dark images because they dominate, but once your mind has flipped over to the white images, the word becomes dominant and that is all you can see. It is now hard to switch back.

Try squinting your eyes and looking at it. It's surprising how that can help you see an image better, isn't it?

Closure

This is often what happens when we look at our environment. We see the dominant image and unless we look more carefully, we completely miss the more important things. Ugliness often dominates and we miss something that is beautiful. We see a confusion of signs and advertising and miss seeing a lovely building or open space beyond. When we begin to really see the beautiful things we might want to try to change the environment so that others can see them too.

As you go home today, take a good look at things. Maybe you will want to try squinting your eyes to see if you can see more. Tomorrow morning let's share some of the beautiful things you see today that you hadn't noticed before.

Instructions for the second exercise

Now I am going to hand out a paper. You are to leave it face down on your desk until I give you the instructions. Don't turn it over until I tell you to.

Again hand out copies of the sheet, "Do You See What You Think You See?"

After we have finished, you can take this sheet home

and try the exercises on your family or friends, if you wish.

There is a paragraph on the sheet. It isn't important what it says. I just want you to read it. Now, you may turn the sheet over and start reading.

After ten to twenty seconds, ask the students to turn the sheet back, face down.

How many times did you see the letter *f*?

Repeat the numbers as they respond.

Two? Four? Seven? Three? One?

Seldom does anyone give the correct number.

Do any of you see another number of *f*'s that hasn't been mentioned?
All right, now turn your sheet back over. How many times does the word *of* appear in the paragraph?

So how many *f*'s are there?

Closure

Sometimes we are conditioned to see certain things. Our mind responds to the letter *f* when it has an "eff" sound but overlooks the letter when it has an "uv" sound.

There are three "eff" sounds and three "uv" sounds in this paragraph, aren't there? However, many of you missed half of them. The same thing can happen when we look at our environment. We may see only the things we expect to see and overlook other things that are just as important.

DO YOU SEE WHAT YOU THINK YOU SEE?

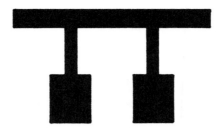

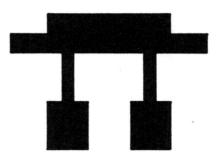

FEATHERY BALLS OF YARN
MAKE FUNNY KINDS OF TOYS
ENJOYED BY FURRY TYPES
OF ANIMALS.

HOW DO YOU FEEL ABOUT YOUR ENVIRONMENT?

Theme

It is often a great revelation to people when they realize that others do not perceive the environment as they do. Environmental decision making would be far more effective if it resulted from the consideration of the opinions of many people. This requires that people have the ability to communicate their feelings to others and an understanding of the differences in individual interpretations. A simple system for evaluating feelings can help people do this.

Learning Objectives

To demonstrate a simple system for evaluating feelings
To develop consideration for the opinions of others

Subject Matter

Social Studies
Language Arts

Time

Forty-five minutes

Vocabulary Words

The hand-out sheet is a vocabulary list.

Materials

Pencils
Copies for each student of the sheet, "How Do You Feel About Your Environment?"

Procedure

Introduce the activity to the students by saying . . .

> As the environment is perceived, feelings develop about, for example, what is . . .
>
> seen—is it pretty or ugly?
> heard—is it loud or quiet?
> smelled—is it good or bad?

tasted—is it sweet or sour?
felt—is it rough or smooth?

Often not much attention is paid to these feelings or time taken to find the right words to describe them. A vocabulary is needed to express these feelings so that they can be communicated to others. A method for recording helps us learn to use a variety of words and provides a way to share these feelings with others.

A format for recording helps us to discover that:
1. Even though the same environment is being observed, the feelings of the individuals about it may be different.
2. Some feel more strongly about an environment than others.
3. Some see more than others.

One way to understand the feelings of others is to use a simple chart to tell others how strong or weak those feelings are.

Hand out the sheet "How Do You Feel About Your Environment?".

This is a list of some adjectives that describe things you might have feelings about in an environment. Each line represents a pair of words that have opposite meanings. In between them is a series of five boxes. At the top there are words heading each column. These are the words that you will use to evaluate the pairs of words. You are to evaluate each pair of words in relation to this room (or any other environment that may be selected). To *evaluate* means to record whether you have very strong feelings about the word description of the environment, rather mild feelings about it, or you don't really care much at all.

For example, let's do the first two words—*ordinary* and *unusual*. Do you feel that this room is very ordinary? Is it like every other room used for this purpose? Or do you think it is somewhat ordinary? Do you think that just a few things about it are different? Maybe you have no feelings, one way or the other, about it. It is just kind of blah and your feelings are neutral. Or do you feel that the room is somewhat unusual or very unusual? You are saying it is different from other rooms used for this purpose and evaluating how much different you think it is. When you have decided how you feel, fill in the box under the proper column heading. You are to fill in only one box in each row. (Show example.)

The words may be new to you or they may have different meanings in relation to this environment, so wait for the explanation of each pair of words before you fill in the next boxes. Don't comment on your selections out loud because we are going to compare them later. You are recording your own special feelings. Don't be concerned about whether your evaluation is right. There are no right or wrong answers. You are just recording what *you feel* right now about this environment.

Go down the word list giving explanations and reminding the students of the degrees of evaluation available for each pair of words.

When the list is completed ask the students to get in groups of not more than four. When the groups are ready say . . .

Each group is to select one person to be a recorder. You will record *only the times* all of the group has exactly the same answer. That means that you will record only the times when you all *agree* about your feelings about this environment. Go down the list together with each person, giving their answer for each line. Don't discuss the answers, just record them. Remember there are no right or wrong answers. Record only the times when you all agree.

When the groups are finished, ask each group to tell you what their score is. Almost always it will be only two or three times that they all agree—maybe none at all!

What did you find out about how people feel about their environment? Right! Hardly anyone feels just the same way. Can you think of some reasons why that is the case?

Typical answers are often . . .

The words mean different things to different people.

We see different things when we look at the room.

We all have different places in mind that we are comparing this room with.

We like different kinds of things.

Suggestions might be . . .

Do you suppose it makes a difference in your evaluation if you don't feel very well at the moment? Would things look better to you on a sunny day than when it is raining? Sometimes it is a good idea to evaluate things at several different times.

What does this tell us needs to be done if we want to

do something different in our room or if we are thinking about participating in changing our environment.

Brainstorm for as many thoughts as possible such as . . .

We need to consider how everybody feels.

We need to know the right words to express our feelings.

Feelings need to be checked at different times, in different weather and so forth.

We will have more ideas if everyone can express feelings.

We will probably never have what one person considers to be the perfect solution.

We probably will have to make compromises or trade-offs to come up with a group decision.

We can do more about changing our environment if everybody has a chance to participate.

Closure

There is so much to see—even in just one room—that people get sort of numb to it all. They don't use their senses to observe what an environment is really like. This sheet is just one way of helping people look carefully at an environment, evaluate what they see, and use some words that will communicate their feelings to others. It is, also, a good format for a person to evaluate different environments that they come in contact with and compare them. After you have done this a few times, it can become a habit. Then you are on the way to becoming an intelligent environmental decision maker.

For practice, use the bottom triangles in the boxes to evaluate another space or to evaluate this room at another time. Add new words if you wish, but remember to always include an opposite of the word.

Using the hand-out sheet as a spelling lesson emphasizes the activity.

HOW DO YOU FEEL ABOUT YOUR ENVIRONMENT?

	VERY	SOMEWHAT	NEUTRAL	SOMEWHAT	VERY	
ORDINARY						UNUSUAL
COMPLEX						SIMPLE
LIGHT						DARK
MODERN						OLD FASHIONED
NOISY						QUIET
UNATTRACTIVE						ATTRACTIVE
SMALL						LARGE
MULTI-PURPOSE						SINGLE PURPOSE
BRIGHT COLORS						SOFT COLORS
OPEN SPACE						CLOSED SPACE
FINISHED						UNFINISHED
SOFT LIGHTING						HARSH LIGHTING
ROOMY						CROWDED
FRIENDLY						UNFRIENDLY
URBAN						RURAL
PUBLIC						PRIVATE
UNIMAGINATIVE						IMAGINATIVE
LIKE						DISLIKE

PICTURES IN YOUR MIND

Theme

Today's world provides an abundance of ready-made images. All that has to be done is to sit back and watch them go by. Response isn't required and, consequently, neither is action. Responsive awareness requires training the mind to pursue all possible and impossible ideas. It takes practice and experience to cultivate creativity and imagination.

Learning Objectives

To expand responsive thought processes
To increase the ability to visualize images
To increase the ability to listen and respond

Subject Matter

Language Arts
Social Studies

Time

Forty-five minutes

Vocabulary Words

visualizing　**design**
images　**visual imaging**

Materials

None

Procedure

Often when we are asked to answer a question, give an opinion, or come up with an idea about something, we can't think of anything to say. Then later on—usually in the middle of the night—we think of exactly the right response. It happens to all of us and it is one of those things that you probably won't outgrow!

However, there are some exercises we can do that will give us practice in letting our minds respond and invent things. It can help us in responding to our envi-

ronment and in **visualizing** what should or should not happen.

Seeing pictures in your mind takes practice and experience. Have you ever stretched out on the grass and looked up at the clouds? You can imagine all sorts of images in them if you concentrate a little bit. What are some **images** that some of you have seen in the clouds?

Let this exchange go on as long as the contributions are good.

Some people see more things than others. It might be because they are more imaginative, but it is more likely to be just that they have practiced more. Just as practice can make you a better ball player, it can make you better at seeing images or pictures.

The clouds provide formations that give you something to start with, but after you practice a little you will be able to see images that are only in your mind. It is a lot like day dreaming, except that you are focusing on a particular thing.

A ball player always warms up before starting to play a game, so we will do some warming up with a ball, too.

Relax. Get very comfortable in your seat. Don't have anything or anyone too close to you because you might not be able to concentrate. Close your eyes so that you can't see anything, but let your eyes feel comfortable too.

In a very lyric voice slowly present the following visual images. Allow enough time after each addition for the students to establish the picture in their minds.

Clear all thoughts from your mind. Don't think about anything else but the middle of your forehead. You are thinking about the spot right between your eyebrows.

It is beginning to bulge out a little; the bulge is getting bigger—bigger—bigger. OH! A ball has popped out! It is a red ball about the size of a ping pong ball.

It has bounced off your desk. It is on the floor, still bouncing up—and—down. The bounces are getting lower—and lower—and lower. It is just barely bouncing now. The red ball is beginning to look sort of funny. It isn't round anymore. It looks kind of squishy. Juice is beginning to—o-o-ze out of it on the floor.

It isn't a round ball at all anymore. It is a flat spot on the floor. The spot is beginning to soak into the floor.

Say quickly . . .

Open your eyes. Maybe you can see the spot before it disappears into the floor!

If most of the students open their eyes and look at the floor, good concentration on the building of the image is indicated.

That was a pretty good warm-up. Now let's see if this game could help you **design** something in the environment. Everybody likes to design houses. A house is an environment. The place you live is probably your most important environment. How creative can you be about designing a home environment?

Get comfortable again and close your eyes. You are standing inside your home. How did you get in? Did you go through the front door? The back door? Did you climb in a window? If you can't get in because all the doors and windows are locked, turn yourself into a mouse. Find a crack to go through. Now you are a mouse inside a room. What does the room look like? Is it square, rectangular, triangular, round, oblong,

hexagonal, octagonal? Is it shaped like a cone, a prism? Go through the other rooms. Now turn yourself from a mouse into a person your own size. Are all the rooms the same height? Do the ceilings slope with the roof? How does the light come in? Through little windows, big ones, skylights?

What colors are the walls? What is on the floors? Is it hard, soft, squishy?

Now think about how you would go outside your home. Walk all around it from the outside. What is it made of, wood, brick, stone, plastic, metal, glass, concrete, tile?

What makes your home special compared to the others in the neighborhood?

Are you walking on grass, a walkway, a deck, gravel, through a flower bed? You had better get out of there! Wipe your feet and go back inside!

What is your very favorite place in the whole home? Where is it? Is it like some other place that you have known? Do you go there alone? Do others know about it? Think of someone that you would like to invite into your favorite place. What would you do? Would you want more people to join you? Do you like your place a lot? Is it a happy place? Is it like a place you have dreamed about? Would you like to change it?

Do you think it is like anyone else's favorite place?

Open your eyes and let's find out.

Put a large sheet of paper up on a good surface for drawing. Have the students share their images of their favorite place in their home environment verbally, but encourage them to come up and draw a picture of it on the paper. This will reinforce the **visual imaging** and expand the thinking of those who are less imaginative.

Closure

That was a wonderful job of visual imaging. It shows how imaginative a mind can be when it is given a chance. TV and movie screens provide us with a wealth of images. If the mind is used to go beyond the image seen on the TV or movie screen, if it is questioning, imagining, and responding creatively to what is being seen, it is then gaining practice and experience in developing a responsive awareness to the environment.

PUTTING IT ON THE DOTTED LINE!

Theme

Systems for organizing environmental observations can provide meaning and understanding. Surveying, charting, categorizing, and prioritizing are rather sophisticated systems for putting information in an order that will increase the ability to see the environment in greater detail. This activity illustrates what is meant by putting something in an order so that the details can be understood and remembered.

Learning Objective

To increase awareness of surroundings
To understand a system for organizing information

Subject Matter

Social Studies
Science
Language Arts

Time

Student: Forty-five minutes to one hour
Teacher: One-half hour to study the lesson plan

Vocabulary Words

image	**visualize**
order	**proportions**
visual communication	**details**
space	**sensory awareness**
design	**sketch**
architecture	**hardline**
observations	

Materials

Pencils and a large sheet of paper for a chart
Copies of Sheets 1a, 2a, 3a, and 4a, "Putting It on the Dotted Line!"

Procedure

Probably most of you have drawn the kind of pictures in which you draw lines between dots and gradually an **image** begins to develop. It is fun to do but it also illustrates something that can help us understand our environment better. The dots are placed in a certain order. When you follow the **order,** you begin to understand what they mean. We can become more aware of what we see if an order is established for seeing the details.

Write the word *awareness* on the chart paper. As you present each idea, add the illustrations shown here to the chart.

We are going to talk about dots for a little bit. You may not have realized how important a dot can be!

For instance, the dot is the smallest unit of **visual communication.** The very smallest speck that you can see with the naked eye will look like a dot. Like this.

●

When you put just two dots together, you have indicated a **space.** Your eye travels over the space between the two dots. How the dots are placed gives both direction and distance for your eye to travel.

|SPACE| /SPACE
●   ●   ●   ●

The dots might be used to indicate a unit of measurement. Dots are often used on maps to show the number of miles between two points.

Put more dots together and you now have a series of spaces. The order in which the dots are placed gives you some kind of a clue to the shape of the spaces.

●   ●   ●
●   ●   ●

Your eye is capable of connecting these dots in several ways. Here are two possibilities.

You will need to have the dots closer together if you are to be sure just what way it is supposed to be done.

The closer the dots are, or the more there are of them, the easier it becomes to understand the shape they are supposed to take. While there still could be several possibilities here, the dots are close enough to make one solution quite obvious. You can see the shape without drawing the lines, because your eyes are able to connect the dots.

Let's see how you can do on connecting some dots!

Hand a copy of Sheet 1a to each student.

Here are just a few dots placed in a special kind of **order.** Draw lines to connect the dots and see what kind of a shape you get. What do you think it might be?

Maybe it is a house, but maybe not.

Hand a copy of Sheet 2a to each student.

Here is another sheet that has more dots to help you see what the image is. See what happens when you join them together.

It may help if you hold the sheet up and sort of squint your eyes at it. Maybe the dots will fall into a pattern.

It would be a good idea if you draw your lines lightly in pencil so you can make changes if you want to.

As they draw the picture, comment . . .

You may be having some trouble figuring out what to do and which way to go. Don't worry about it. This is just for fun so do the best you can.

When most of the students are about finished, ask . . .

What would make this easier for you? (Knowing where to start, which direction to go, to have arrows or numbers to follow.) Those things help to establish the order for the dots, don't they?

Hand out a copy of Sheet 3a for each student.

You will notice that there are numbers for you to follow on this sheet.

Now you have enough information about the order of the dots to be able to develop the image. Draw the lines in this picture and compare it with your others. It is looking better now that you know more about what to do? Do you know what the picture is?

Yes, it might be a church or a bank. Many of them look kind of like this but that isn't what the **design** was used for originally. It is something that we have adapted from our Greek and Roman heritage. What do you think this kind of building design was used for?

You have made some good suggestions and some of you were pretty close. It was the design for a temple either dedicated to one of the gods or as a place to store money and treasures. Since our country was founded on the Greek principles of government and philosophy, it is natural that we adapted their **architecture** as well. We have often made churches like their religious temples or banks like the places where they stored their treasures.

Hand out a copy of Sheet 4a for each student.

Here is a drawing that is similar to the one you have been working on. It is St. Peter's Church in New York City. Compare this drawing with yours. Make corrections or additions to your drawing from your **observations** of the picture. See if you don't notice much more of the detail on the drawing because you have worked with the dots and tried to **visualize** the image of the picture.

Closure

Dots can be a helpful system for you to use when you want to make a map or draw a picture. If you want to get the **proportions** right—that means if you want the sizes of things to match each other—it helps to dot in the locations and shapes of all the things in the drawing first. That way you can look it over and make changes before you draw all the lines in. Your drawing will turn out a lot better than it does when you start out at one corner and then find that you have run out of room when you get to the other side of the sheet!

This system for putting what you see in order also helps you look much more carefully at the **details.** It increases your **sensory awareness** to your environment. It makes you see much more. That helps you to enjoy and care for your environment more.

Use this system to draw a picture of your house or some other building and bring it in tomorrow. Remember to dot in the outline first. You won't need to put in as many dots, but put in enough to get the details in order and to make the proportions in your drawing look better. **Sketch** it in lightly first, make corrections and then **hardline** your drawing.

Let's make an exhibit of all of these drawings that you did today and compare them with the ones you bring in tomorrow.

PUTTING IT ON THE DOTTED LINE... SHEET 1B

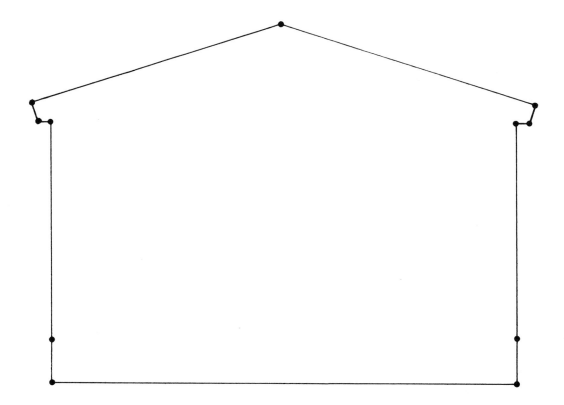

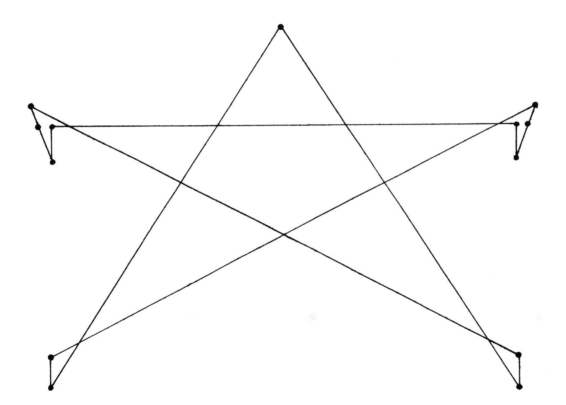

PUTTING IT ON THE DOTTED LINE... SHEET 2A

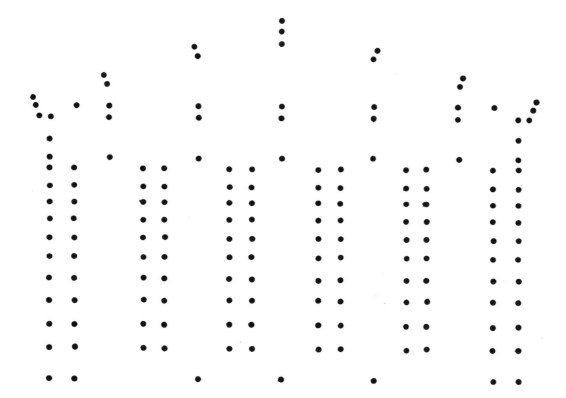

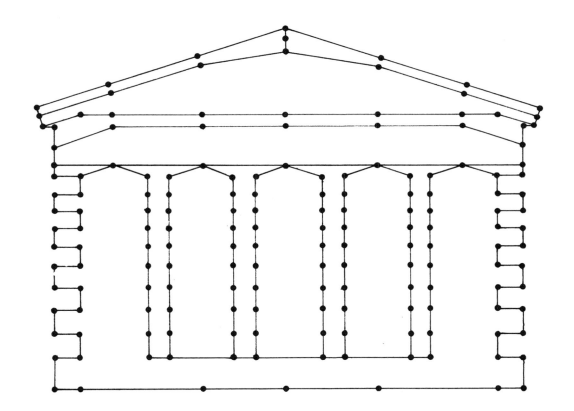

PUTTING IT ON THE DOTTED LINE...
SHEET 2C

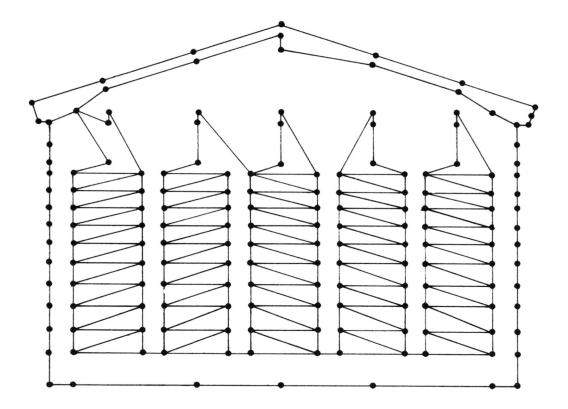

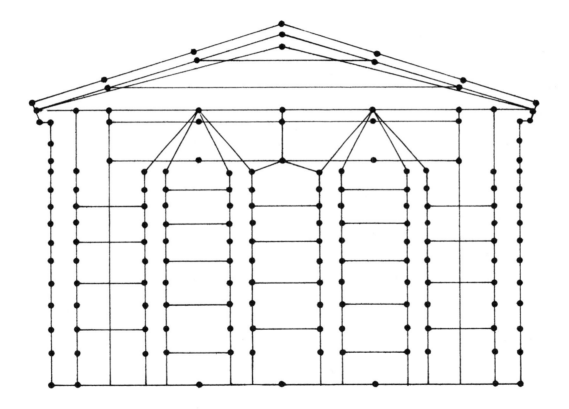

PUTTING IT ON THE DOTTED LINE...
SHEET 3A

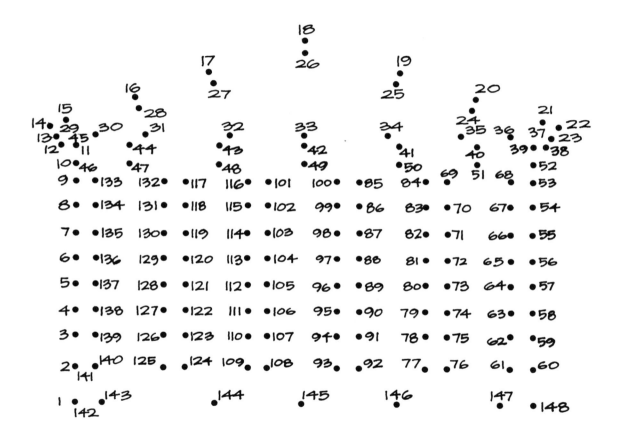

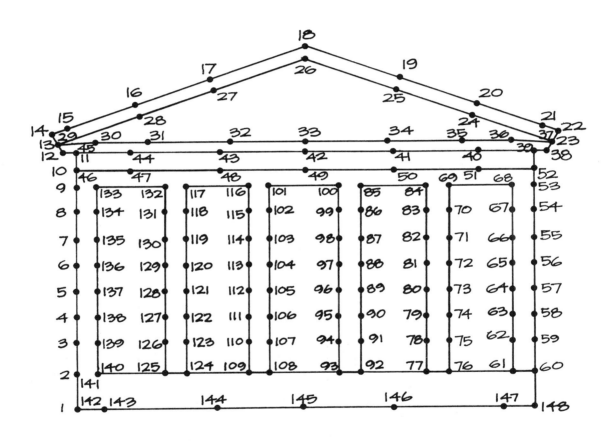

PUTTING IT ON THE DOTTED LINE...
SHEET 3C

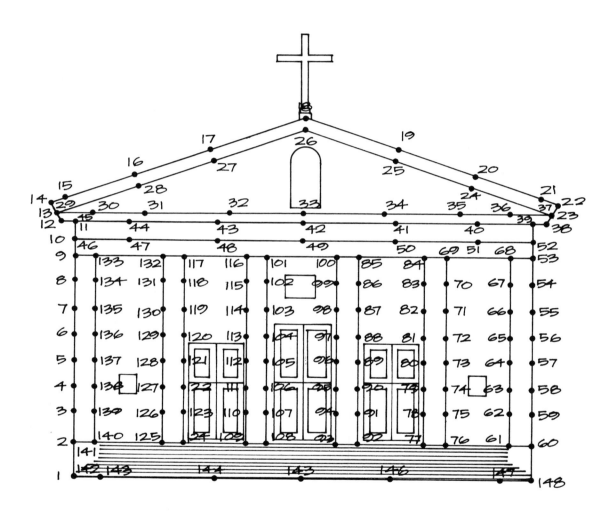

PUTTING IT ON THE DOTTED LINE...
SHEET 4

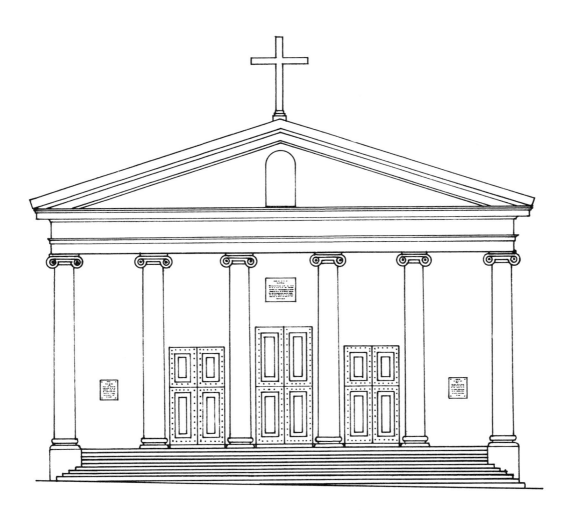

PLAYING A BUILDING

Theme

Most of our perceptions of our environment focus on visual observations. However, our sensitivity can be greatly enhanced if we train our other senses to be utilized also. The world is full of sounds for us to hear. Music is a way of putting these sounds in an order that increases our sensory awareness. This activity relates the concepts of musical composition to similar ones in design composition.

Learning Objectives

To gain an understanding of the concepts of artistic composition
To increase sensory perception

Subject Matter

Music
Science
Art

Time

Forty-five minutes to one hour

Vocabulary Words

systems	**repetition**
order	**variation**
composition	**symmetrically balanced**
balance	**details**
rhythm	**asymmetrically balanced**
symmetry	**design**

Materials

Overhead projector
Record player
Selected records
Copies for each student of Sheets 1–6

Procedure

We are going to listen to some records and look at some pictures of buildings to help us become more aware of our environment and to understand how it is having an effect on all of us, all of the time. We need many **systems** for sensing what is really there to be seen and experiencing what we see. That is the first step we have to take, if we are to feel a sense of responsibility for our environment. Maybe we would like to change it or maybe we would like to keep it from changing.

Musical notes are a system for putting the sounds we hear in an **order.** When some notes are placed in certain order they make pleasant sounds when played on an instrument or sung. Others don't sound very nice. Some of them can really hurt our ears in the same way a bad environment can bother us.

When musical sounds are connected together, they form a **composition.** If the composition is pleasing to the ears, it will probably have such things as **balance, rhythm, symmetry, repetition,** and **variation.** A well designed building or work of art will have these same kinds of qualities. Looking at a building in relation to music is a system for enhancing our awareness, both of sounds and of buildings.

Let's see if we can "Play a Building." By that we mean relating the composition of the building to the musical composition.

Show the example on Sheet 1 on the overhead projector.

Here is a drawing of a Greek temple and a couple of simple musical scores that might go with it. A Greek temple is a very **symmetrically balanced** building with repetition and rhythm in the **details.**

Play a record that has these qualities. While it is playing, place Sheet 2 on the projector.

When the record is finished, place Sheet 3 on the overhead projector.

This is a house from the Victorian period. It is quite different from the temple. There is a lot of rhythm and variation in this building. There is some fantasy in it, too. The building is balanced but the sides aren't the same. This building is **assymmetrically balanced.** It is what would be called a very romantic building. It would sound something like this.

Play a romantic composition. While it is playing, place Sheet 4 on the projector.

When the record is finished, place Sheet 5 on the overhead projector.

> Here is a block of row houses. They each are repetition of one **design.** The roofs, porches, and chimneys seem to be marching along in a formation like soldiers, don't they? They probably would sound something like this.

Play a simple march composition. While it is playing, place Sheet 6 on the projector.

> What buildings are used for makes us have feelings about them that can be expressed in music, too. What would a prison sound like?

Have the students sing sounds or songs that they think represent a prison building.

How about a concert hall?

An amusement park should be fun to do.

An office building?

A fast food restaurant?

A church?

Perhaps the students could be divided in groups and assigned the different buildings. Give the groups five minutes to decide what they are going to do and then have them present it to the rest of the class. Suggest that they combine music and drawing or cut out pictures.

PLAYING A BUILDING
SHEET 1

PLAYING A BUILDING
SHEET 2

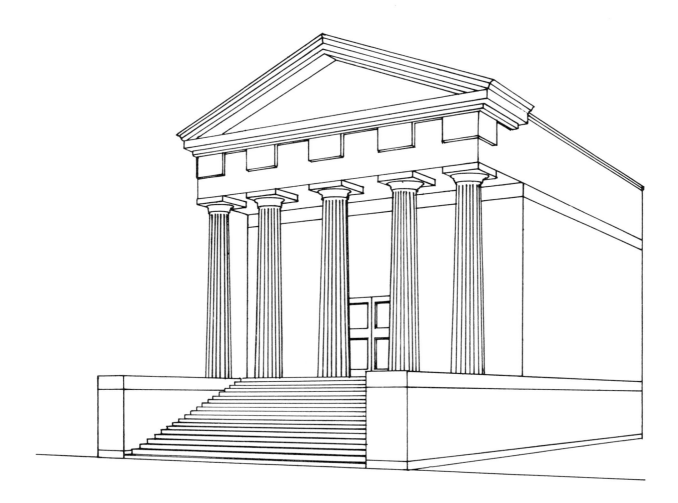

PLAYING A BUILDING
SHEET 3

PLAYING A BUILDING
SHEET 4

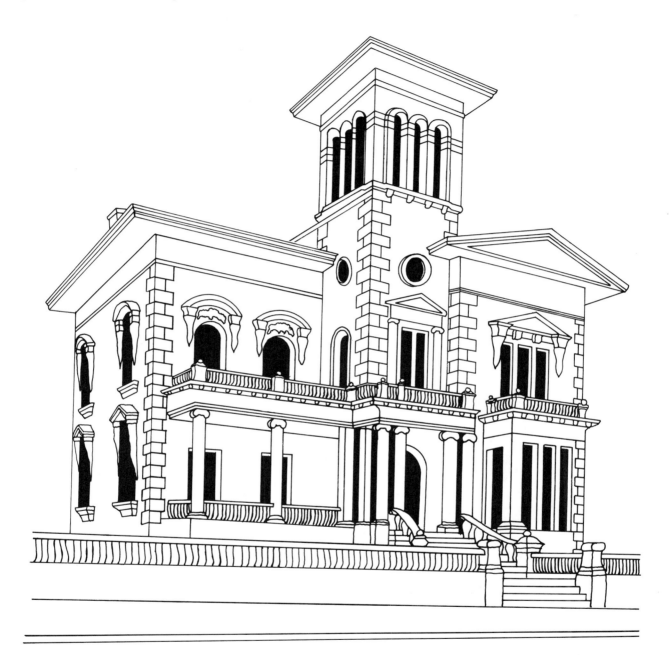

PLAYING A BUILDING
SHEET 5

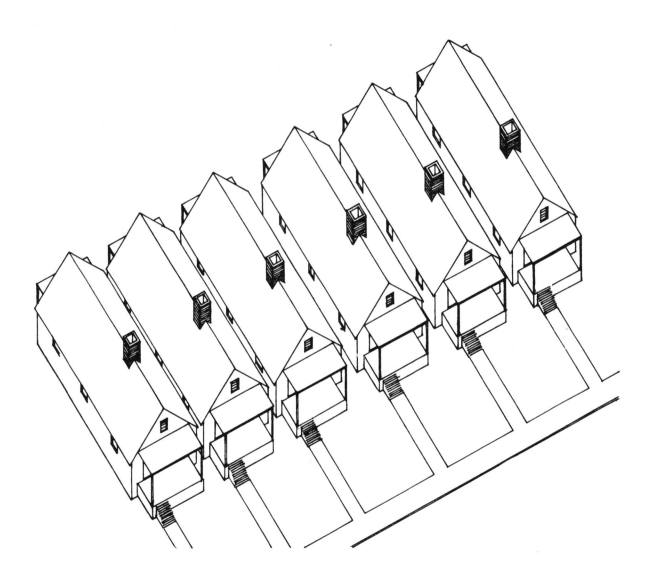

PLAYING A BUILDING
SHEET 6

WHAT DO YOU SEE HERE?

Theme

Putting objects that are seen in the environment in an orderly form improves one's ability to perceive them. Drawing a plan of the classroom and using a checklist provide two means of organizing observations and thus increasing perception of the space.

Learning Objectives

To increase visual perception
To become aware of numbers, sizes, and the spatial relationships of objects

Subject Matter

Science
Math
Art
Language arts

Time

Forty-five minutes to one hour

Vocabulary Words

floor plan   **order**
observation   **space**
checklist   **spatial relationships**
decision-making process **detail**
key   **visual communication**
scale   **sketch**
symbols

Materials

12″ × 18″ sheets of light-colored construction paper or sheets of butcher paper
Pencils
Narrow-tip felt pens
Copies for each of the students of the sheets "Symbols to Use in Drawing a Floor Plan I-III", "How to Measure a Room", and "Floor Plan Checklist."

A set of architect's plans for the school, if available. Do not show them to the students until after they have finished their plan.

Preparation

Cut paper to the proper size to represent the room size at a scale of 1/2″ = 1′0″. For example, if the room is 24′ × 36′, the 12″ × 18″ paper is just right. A 20′ × 32′ room will need a sheet 10″ × 16″. If your classroom is not a rectangular shape of approximately this size or is a different shape, measure it and adjust the paper size. Students are upset if the size of the paper is not appropriate for the size of the room.

Procedure

In the classroom session:

Explain to the students that they are going to draw a floor plan of their classroom.

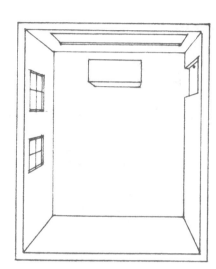

> A **floor plan** is like a map of the room. What you see on a map are all the things on the floor that a bird would see if it were flying right above the room and there were no ceiling. Stand up and stretch your arms out to your sides. Imagine that you are such a bird and you are flying around over this room at the level of your outstretched arms. What you will show on your map, or floor plan, of this room are all the things that the bird would see that are below the level of your arms.
>
> To make this drawing you will need to use your ability to look around you and draw what you see. You will be drawing from your **observations**. You will have to carefully notice what is in the room, where things are located in relation to each other, how far apart things are, and what the size of each thing is compared to other things in the room.
>
> It is often helpful to check a list to be sure that you remember everything. Here is a **checklist** to help you with your drawing of the floor plan.

Write the list on the board or on a chart.

1. The objects—desks, tables, windows, doors, etc.
2. Their location in the room
3. The distance they are from each other
4. Their size compared to each other

> Now you will need to know how you are going to draw these things on your floor plan, won't you? When you look at a map, what do you often find on it that helps you understand the map?

Press with questions until you get the answer.

> (A **key**.)
>
> Right. It helps if you have a key. A key is a way of

putting things that we see in an **order** that helps us to understand them and to communicate them so others will also understand them.

Have sheets of scale-sized paper ready in several colors (light enough for the drawing to show up well). Some students will be quite good at these spatial relationships and will be concerned if the size of the paper is too far off the scale. Ask the students to select the color they would like to have for their drawing. As they are making their selections, question them about the reasons for their choice. This provides another opportunity to emphasize the individual **decision-making process**.

This sheet of paper is about the right size to represent the size of this room, if you are drawing your plan at a *scale* of one-half inch to one foot.

The sheets approximate the size of the average classroom at this scale well enough for the purpose.

We can't make a drawing as big as this room. What we usually do when we draw a picture of something large is to reduce it to fit on the piece of paper you have. If your drawing turns out well—if it looks like the thing that you are trying to draw—it means that you have reduced all the parts of the object by the same amount. Sometimes we use the expression "scaling a thing up or down." Sometimes we do this just by careful observation with our eyes, but if we want to do it very accurately, we measure it with a ruler. This is called "making a drawing to scale." It takes more time but you will have a drawing that is exactly like the object or place you are drawing. The only difference will be in the size. So this sheet of paper is about the right size for you to make a floor plan of this room at a **scale** of 1/2 inch equals 1 foot.

At this point you may want to refer to Rulers at Various Scales (page 182), which should help students in their measurements.

Write on the board 1/2" = 1'0". Hand out copies of the sheets "Symbols to Use in Drawing a Floor Plan" I-III and "How to Measure a Room".

The **symbols** on Sheet II are drawn at the scale of one-half inch to one foot, so they are the right size for you to use on your floor plan. Look carefully at the symbols and then at the things in the room. If your plan is going to be accurate—if it is going to tell others who look at it exactly what this room looks like—you will need to draw each object in the correct size and location in relation to the size of the whole room. You will need to notice the size of the spaces between the objects, too. Compare the sizes of those **spaces** with the sizes of the objects to figure out how big to draw them. Look at the door and then at the symbol for the door. That is how a door looks at a scale of 1/2" = 1'0". Look at a window and at the symbol for a window. Now look at the space between the windows and compare it with the size of the windows. That will help you decide how much space to leave on your drawing.

Remember that you are looking straight down on the room. You will only see the top of the counters, not the doors below. The sink will just be a rectangle. The windows will just be lines as though you see only the edge of the glass. The doors will be openings in the walls. Will the walls be just one line? Why not? What would you see if you sliced through a wall? There might be wood or concrete block between the wall finishes on either side, so you will draw two lines. Walls are about six inches thick, so how far apart will your lines be? (One quarter of an inch.) What will happen when two rooms are next to each other? Do you have two walls? (No, only one wall that both rooms share.)

It will probably take a little experimenting to get things in the proper locations and in the proper sizes, so you should use a pencil and lightly **sketch** things in first. Sketch everything that you see on the floor of the room that does not move. The symbols you have on Sheets I and II are all of things that don't move.

It will make it easier for you if you place your paper on your desk in the same position as the room is to your desk. Now locate the door through which you enter the room and draw it in. Remember to think about how big the door should be and how close to the wall. This will help you in locating everything else.

As the students draw, go around pointing out the sizes of objects on the symbol sheet and encouraging them to look at the actual object and to get the sizes correct. Remind the students to sketch lightly so they will be able to make corrections. Some students are far more adept in **spatial relationships** than others. Remember that the value of the exercise is in the observations made, not in the quality of the drawing.

When they are about finished and feel satisfied with their pencil sketches, ask them to start going over them with a narrow-tipped felt pen, one color only. When they have completed that task, say . . .

You probably think that, because you are here most of the day, this room is so familiar to you that you could draw it without even looking! We often think that about environments that are very familiar to us. That is a problem about environmental awareness. We take it for granted and don't stop to really see what is there.

Let's see if you really see the environment in this classroom. Let's see if you have forgotten anything.

Hand out the sheet, "Floor Plan Check List."

A plan is a good way to put things in order. A checklist is another good way to organize things and to be sure that you don't forget anything.

To use this checklist you will have to do some counting first. Go down the list. Count the number of each of the objects listed and write the number in the blank.

Go down the list with the students. Have various students count the different objects to provide a check. Be sure they are recording the correct number in the proper blank.

Now you have a checklist with the correct numbers of each of the things in the room. Count the number of each of the objects that you have on your drawing. Write the number in the blank alongside the first number. If the numbers don't match, look around and see where the objects are that you left out. Maybe you will have too many of some things and will have to find out which ones to take out.

Let's start with the doors. How many doors are there in the room? Do you have them on your plan? Are they in the right location?

If you don't have the right number or you haven't drawn it in the right location, take a different colored felt pen and correct your drawing. If you have too many, figure out which to take out.

It may be helpful to have the students work in pairs on this so they can help each other. Go down each item on the checklist in the same manner. When completed, compare with the drawings.

What things have we left out of our plan? Right. The furniture. We have a plan of all the things that don't move. That is the way an architect's plan is drawn. We haven't drawn in the things that do move because they don't always stay in the same place.

Another day we will cut out the furniture pieces using our checklist to get the right numbers. Then we will arrange them on our plan as the room is now. Then we will rearrange them to make a new plan of the room indicating some changes that you would like to make.

(Use the ½″ = 1′0″ pieces of Sheet III as patterns for cutting out the required numbers of each piece. Color coding the pieces illustrates another method for organizing observations.)

Note: This is a very popular activity but we have found that it takes too long for one session. Doing the drawing of things that don't move in one day is enough. Cutting out the furniture pieces then allows manipulation of them for rearrangement more conveniently than making drawings, and this becomes another session.

Closure

Initiate a class discussion about ways to increase the powers of observation and other ways of recording what is seen as a means of increasing perception.

> You have noticed things about your classroom that you were not really aware of before. When we are too familiar with something, we often don't really look at it with any feeling or understanding. When we take a closer look, we often begin to question why things are the way they are and where they are. Sometimes we realize that there are things that we like very much and we would like to keep them. Sometimes we realize that there are things that we would like to change.

Show the students an architect's plan of the school, if available. Help them find the classroom they have just drawn. It will probably be in a different scale from the one they used. Smaller scales are used for overall floor plans and larger ones for showing details. Discuss the importance of accuracy in this kind of **visual communication.**

SYMBOLS TO USE IN DRAWING A FLOOR PLAN I

- AN ARCHITECT'S FLOOR PLAN USED TO BUILD A BUILDING SHOWS ONLY THE THINGS THAT DON'T MOVE....
- A FLOOR PLAN IS A BIRD'S—EYE VIEW LOOKING STRAIGHT DOWN.

· STRETCH YOUR ARMS OUT LIKE THE BIRD'S WINGS · A FLOOR PLAN SHOWS ONLY WHAT IS IN THE SPACE BELOW YOUR ARM'S LEVEL.

3'-6" TO 4'

- THIS IS A FLOOR PLAN SYMBOL KEY.
- IT IS DRAWN AT A SCALE OF 1/4" = 1'-0"!

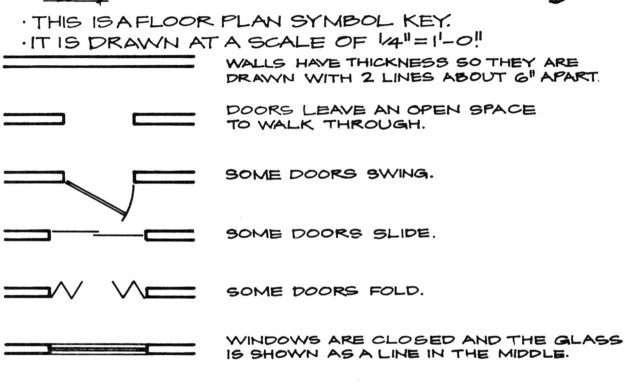

WALLS HAVE THICKNESS SO THEY ARE DRAWN WITH 2 LINES ABOUT 6" APART.

DOORS LEAVE AN OPEN SPACE TO WALK THROUGH.

SOME DOORS SWING.

SOME DOORS SLIDE.

SOME DOORS FOLD.

WINDOWS ARE CLOSED AND THE GLASS IS SHOWN AS A LINE IN THE MIDDLE.

CHALK AND BULLETIN BOARDS ARE SHOWN AS A LINE ON THE SIDE OF THE WALL.

CUPBOARDS AND CLOSETS ARE SHOWN THIS WAY.

SINK

ONLY THE TOPS OF COUNTERS AND SINKS ARE SHOWN.

SYMBOLS TO USE IN DRAWING A FLOOR PLAN II

- DESIGNERS USUALLY DRAW ROOM ARRANGEMENT PLANS AT A SCALE OF ½"=1'0."
- THEY LIKE TO CUT OUT FURNITURE PIECES AND TRY THEM OUT ON THE FLOOR PLAN — ¼"=1'0" PIECES ARE HARD TO HANDLE.
- THIS IS A FLOOR PLAN SYMBOL KEY.
- IT IS DRAWN AT A SCALE OF ½"=1'0."

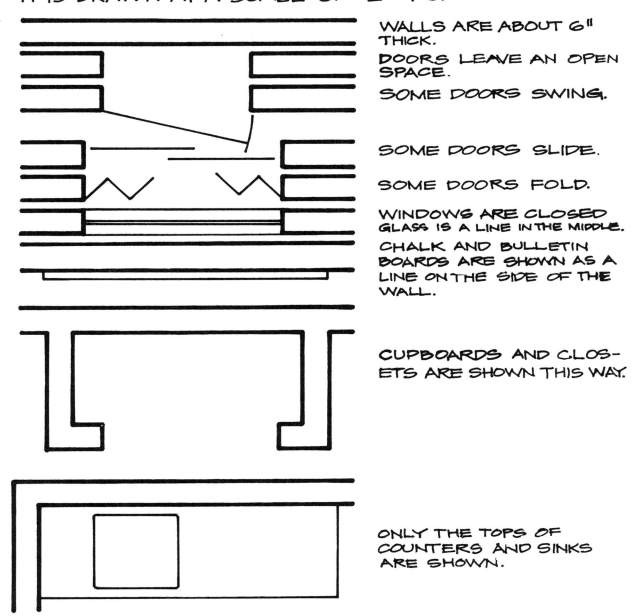

WALLS ARE ABOUT 6" THICK.

DOORS LEAVE AN OPEN SPACE.

SOME DOORS SWING.

SOME DOORS SLIDE.

SOME DOORS FOLD.

WINDOWS ARE CLOSED GLASS IS A LINE IN THE MIDDLE.

CHALK AND BULLETIN BOARDS ARE SHOWN AS A LINE ON THE SIDE OF THE WALL.

CUPBOARDS AND CLOSETS ARE SHOWN THIS WAY.

ONLY THE TOPS OF COUNTERS AND SINKS ARE SHOWN.

SYMBOLS TO USE IN DRAWING A FLOOR PLAN III

A ROOM ARRANGEMENT FLOOR PLAN INCLUDES ALL THE THINGS IN A SPACE THAT CAN BE MOVED.

THIS KEY SHOWS THE MOVABLE THINGS AT TWO SCALES.

SCALE ¼"=1'-0"

| DESKS |

24" x 20" OR 30" x 24"
STUDENTS DESKS

SCALE ½"=1'-0"

| DESKS |

THE FIRST DIMENSION IS ALWAYS THE WIDTH.

| DESK |

5'-0" x 2'-6"
TEACHER'S DESK

| DESK |

| CH'R | | CH'R |

16" x 14"
STUDENT'S CHAIR
18" x 16"
TEACHER'S CHAIR

| CHAIR | | CHAIR |

3'-0" 4' 5' 6' 7' 8'

3'-0" 4' 5' 6' 7' 8'

12" BOOKCASES COME IN MANY WIDTHS.

| TABLES |

5'-0" & 6'-0" x 2'-6"
WORK TABLES

| TABLES |

FLOOR PLAN CHECK LIST

OBJECT	NUMBER IN ROOM
DOORS	_____
WINDOWS	_____
DESKS	_____
CHAIRS	_____
RECTANGULAR TABLES	_____
ROUND TABLES	_____
BOOKCASES	_____
COUNTERS	_____
SINKS	_____
CLOSETS	_____
WASTEBASKETS	_____
OTHER THINGS	
_____	_____
_____	_____
_____	_____
_____	_____

HOW TO MEASURE A ROOM

WHAT MEASUREMENTS TO TAKE AND HOW TO SHOW THEM ON A FLOOR PLAN

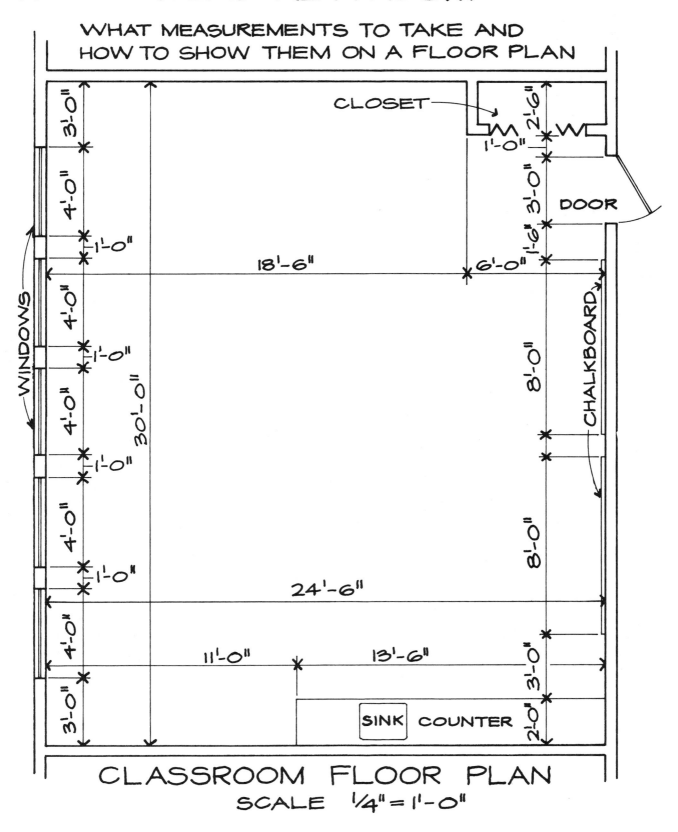

CLASSROOM FLOOR PLAN
SCALE 1/4" = 1'-0"

2 THE COMMUNITY WHERE YOU LIVE

INTRODUCTION

Theme

This series of activities is designed to help students gain an understanding of a process for observing, recording, and analyzing information about the built environment. The over-all focus is on how this information relates to the need for background in making good environmental decisions .

Any of the activities can be done separately, but as a series they provide a comprehensive process for viewing a community. Repeated in different community areas, they can offer a format for comparison.

The Activities

1. Have You Ever Seen. . . ?
2. Sketching in the Community
3. Texture Rubbings
4. Hanging the Show
5. Scavenger Hunting in the Community
6. Interviewing Community Resources

These activities provide things to look for, ways to focus on what is seen, to develop appreciation, to make group decisions, and ways to communicate a message.

Curriculum Areas

Social Studies   through learning a process for understanding the community and recognition of the individual's responsibility to gain a background for participation in decision making

Math   through utilizing counting, graphing, and charting as a means of understanding a community

Science   through observing, recording, and analyzing techniques

Art   through drawing and mounting, spatial arrangement and observation, and the development of appreciation

Language Arts   through word recognition and understanding and group discussion skills

Health   through focusing on the five senses

Where

With the increase in financial and energy restrictions, field trips of any distance may become increasingly difficult for the schools. While getting students to know as large an area as possible is desirable, any of these activities can be done within the school or the surrounding area within walking distance. The process could be done in relation to some community being studied in social studies to provide the basis for comparison.

Why

With the acceleration of change in our communities, many citizens have become concerned and are taking an active role in directing that change.

Citizen planning organizations are becoming important in the development of comprehensive plans and neighborhood associations are being formed to monitor change and preserve community character.

Many people are not aware of the possiblities for individual impact or how to go about developing a sense of community in order to understand the problems and strengths.

This sense of community and the individual's responsibility can begin to form at a very young age. This group of activities in The Community Where You Live provides some ways to begin. They each reinforce a process involving group participation, focus, action involvement, visual communications, and group decision making.

Extension

Brainstorming an idea and developing an actual project for the school or the community is strong reinforcement for the students of the premise that the individual can have an impact on the community.

It is also an excellent way to get parent and community interest and involvement in the school.

Bibliography

The Image of the City by Kevin Lynch, MIT Press. Cambridge, Mass., 1960.

Presents a readable theory of the way people perceive the city. It identifies distinctive environmental elements (paths, districts, edges, nodes, landmarks) and discusses how we are affected by our perception of them.

The Child in the City by Colin Ward, Pantheon Books, New York, 1978.

A probing and caring exploration of the ways in which the city can serve or fail children.

HAVE YOU EVER SEEN...?

Theme

The type of buildings that people build tells a good deal about the character of their communities. In order to become aware of buildings, it is more interesting if they are not only recognized visually, but can be referred to in architectural terms.

Learning Objectives

To increase visual perception
To develop the ability to identify and categorize objects

Subject Matter

Social studies

Science

Art

Language Arts

Time

Forty-five minutes before classroom session
Forty-five minutes in class

Vocabulary Words

details	molding
column	roof pitch
colonnade	architecture
Doric	square
Ionic	round
Corinthian	rectangle
arch	triangle
arcade	shaft
paneled	capital
pediment	base
portico	

Materials

Copies for each student of the sheet, "Have You Ever Seen. . . ?"

Felt pens, narrow-line

Old magazines, particularly home decorating and architectural, one for each student

Magazine cut-outs with examples from the handout sheet outlined on them (see pages 60-62)

Masking tape

Large sheet of butcher paper

Books on architecture

Procedure

Hand out the sheet, "Have Your Ever Seen. . . ?"

Go over details, pointing out the examples on the pictures that have been outlined. Ask them to repeat the words with you.

Ask the students to each get a magazine and to begin to find examples of all the things on the hand-out sheet. When they have found an example, ask them to outline it on the picture in felt pen, then to check it off in the proper square on the hand-out sheet. Ask them to try to find examples for every square on the sheet.

When most of them are finishing, mark headings on the butcher paper—**Columns, Arches, Doors, Windows,** and **Roofs.**

Have them tape their examples under the proper heading.

Explain to the students that:

Buildings tell us a great deal about the community and the people in it. However, there are so many buildings all around us that we often don't pay much attention to how they look individually. If we have some particular things to look for, it helps us become aware of how one building is different from another and why we like some of them better than others.

The design of buildings is an art. Does anyone know what it is called?

Yes, it is called **architecture** and you have been working with the architectural names for things that you may see.

With a little practice you will be able to identify them on all the buildings that you see. That will help you know more about buildings and through that you will gain more knowledge of your community.

Initiate a discussion about the similarities, differences, preferences, etc., using the student pictures as a focus.

Have a table with architectural books for the students.

Closure

With all these examples, it should be much easier for you to recognize these **details** wherever you may see them. You have outlined the shapes and now I think you should be able to draw them yourselves. Take the

sheet home with you and tomorrow bring back three drawings of different details that you have found in your home. Then we will add them to the exhibit. They don't *have* to be things that are on the sheet. When you begin to know a few details, you will find that you begin to see many more.

HAVE YOU EVER SEEN.....?

HERE ARE SOME TYPICAL ARCHITECTURAL FEATURES YOU CAN EASILY FIND IF YOU START LOOKING AROUND MOST ANYWHERE - CHECK THE SQUARE WHEN YOU FIND ONE.

☐

CAPITAL

SHAFT

BASE

A COLUMN

☐ TOGETHER COLUMNS FORM A COLONADE.

THE TOP OF A COLUMN IS CALLED A CAPITAL.

THE MOST COMMON ONES ARE

☐ DORIC   ☐ IONIC   ☐ CORINTHIAN

☐ AN ARCH

☐ TOGETHER THEY FORM AN ARCADE.

☐ A PANELED DOOR

DOOR WITH A ROOF AND COLUMNS IS A PORTICO. ☐

THE TRIANGLE ROOF IS A PEDIMENT. ☐

THE ARCH IS A FAN LIGHT OR MOULDING. ☐

WINDOW MAY BE:

SQUARE   ROUND   TRIANGULAR   RECTANGULAR
☐   ☐   ☐   ☐

THEY MIGHT HAVE:

LEADED GLASS ☐
STAINED GLASS ☐

ROOFS MAY BE:

PITCHED   FLAT
☐   ☐   ☐   ☐   ☐

LEARNING THESE ARCHITECTURAL TERMS CAN HELP YOU TALK ABOUT WHAT YOU SEE —

SKETCHING IN THE COMMUNITY

Theme

One of the most easily available places to experience the built environment is in the community where the students go to school and live. Drawing pictures of what is seen requires focusing on the details and sharpens environmental perception.

Learning Objectives

To develop perceptual skills by recording environmental details
To develop and improve drawing skills by working from real-life observations

Subject Matter

Social Studies
Art
Language Arts

Time

Prior to the classroom session:
One hour to select and investigate an area for the sketching walk and to develop questions for the classroom discussion.

Time to get parents to help, number depending on the grade level.

The classroom session:
Fifteen minutes for class discussion
Thirty to sixty minutes for the sketching walk
Fifteen minutes for follow-up class discussion

Vocabulary Words

rural	**changing**
suburban	**new development**
urban	**preservation**
apartment	**conservation**
duplex	**citizen participation**
single family home	**details**
mobile home	**sketch**
farm	**density**
construction	**comprehensive planning**
remodel	**aesthetic appreciation**
established	

Materials

Sketch pads or sheets of paper to fit the boards
Clip or cake boards (see Clipboards for Status, page 191)
Pencils and narrow-line felt pens
1 or 2 pocket pencil sharpeners
Copies for each student and adult leader of the sheet, "Have You Ever Seen. . . ?" (see previous activity)

Preparation

Prior to the classroom session:

Select an area near the school, perferably a quiet one to minimize distractions and traffic concerns, but one with some diversity. Walk through the area making notes on interesting features and building details that can be discussed and observed later.

Having the students do the activity, Have You Ever Seen. . . ? before this recommended.

Procedure

Before starting on the walk:

Adult Helpers:

Study a copy of this whole lesson plan and the hand-out sheet and listen to the class discussion. This will aid in making relevant comments during the walk.

Teacher:

Hand out copies of the sheet, "Have You Ever Seen. . . ?" and go over the pictures and terms.

Initiate a class discussion that will familiarize the students with some additional terms that architects and planners use through questions such as:

How would you describe this community where you live and go to school? Write the words **rural, suburban**, and **urban** on a chart.

What kind of a place do you live in? Write **apartment, duplex, single family home, mobile home, farm** on the chart.

In the area where you live are the places all about the same age? How old do you think the oldest is? The newest?

Are some of them not finished? Still under **construction**? Being **remodeled**?

What does this tell you about this community? Write **established, changing**, and **new development** on the chart.

Does the place in which you live look much like the others in the area? What are some of the things that make it different?

Does the time in which a place was built make a difference in how it looks? Should we try to save old places? Write **preservation** and **conservation**.

Is the community crowded? Are there vacant lots? Open fields? Woods?

Is the space being used up? Write **density** and **comprehensive planning**.

Is this something that we should be concerned about? How could we go about doing something? Write **citizen participation**.

The sketching walk can now be introduced as a way to learn to use a valuable tool for looking carefully at the environment in order to see more of what is really there to see.

Suggest that. . .

> If you are going to become good citizens, who are concerned about your community and want to make good decisions about how it is cared for and changed, you will need to know a lot about it. Citizens are only effective when they are informed. In fact, a lot of harm can be done by people who don't know what they are talking about. Before you can do anything about caring for the environment, or anything else for that matter, you have to know what it is you want to do.
>
> A good way to begin to find that out is to learn to really see what is there, to learn to see the **details**. A camera is a good tool for focusing on details, but you don't always have one with you. You do always have your hands with you, however, and if you work on learning how to draw the things you see, you will soon find that you are seeing a lot more. That will be the first step toward knowing more about your community.

Drawing a picture not only helps you to see more but it often helps others to understand what you are seeing more easily than when you try to explain it with words.

A picture is also a valuable tool for sending a message.

Now, let's take a walk and see if we can find some things to **sketch**. Each of you take a clip board and fasten the sheet of details you have been given and several pieces of paper on it. If you refer to the sheet as you walk along, it will help you get started finding things to sketch. You will need pencils and pens so that you can try drawing with both of them.

Divide the class in groups and assign the adult helpers. Tell them where you are going and what the time limit will be. As the class walks along in the selected area, the leaders should be calling attention to details, asking the students questions about what they are seeing and referring to the hand-out sheet to help the students to recognize the details.

After they have had time to look for awhile, ask them to select something they want to draw. They may want to circle back to something seen earlier.

Have them find a place to sit down where they can draw comfortably.

Encourage them not to try to draw too much. Maybe the first drawing should be just a doorway or window.

Suggest that they draw the outline of the form first, then look carefully at the specific details before adding them to the drawing.

Accept no "I can't draw" excuses. Anyone can draw a rectangle or a square and embellish it according to what is there to be seen.

Younger children can be encouraged to look for repetition of geometric shapes, patterns, etc.

Ask the students to do at least one drawing each in pencil and in felt pen.

Encourage doing several quick sketches, although be sure that the major details are included. Insist that they keep looking until they have seen most of what is there.

As they are drawing, the leaders should move among the students, reminding them of the terms that were used on the hand-out and in the discussion so that these words will become part of their vocabulary.

Upon returning to the classroom:

Do one or all of the following:

Have them hang up the drawing that they liked best. Be sure to emphasize that these are sketches done to catch an idea; they are not meant to be finished drawings.

Initiate a class discussion. . .

What did you see that you might have missed if you hadn't been making a sketch?

How can this help you know more about the community?

Go back over the words that have been written on the board and discuss them in relation to the area of the walk.

Closure

If you keep looking at and sketching things that you see, you will gradually find your appreciation of the environment changing. When you look at many kinds of similar things, you begin to see that some of them look better than others. There is a word for this kind of appreciation. It is called **aesthetic appreciation**. (Add this to the list on the chart.)

It is important for us to develop aesthetic appreciation. It gives us a good feeling inside to be aware of beautiful things. It also makes us care more about what happens to the environment in which we live. Sketching becomes easier as you practice, so this week turn in three more sketches of things that you have seen around your neighborhood or on the way home from school.

TEXTURE RUBBINGS

Theme

Becoming aware of textures that are seen all around helps us to gain an understanding of the structures and materials that are found in the built environment. Making rubbings of these textures encourages a focus on small detail.

Learning Objectives

To gain awareness of the environment through the use of the senses of sight and touch.
To recognize variations and aesthetic qualities that are inherent in the textures of materials.

Subject Matter

Science
Art
Language Arts

Time

Prior to the classroom session:
Thirty minutes to make rubbing examples

The classroom session:
Forty-five minutes for doing the rubbings
Forty-five minutes for developing the display

Vocabulary Words

textures   **relief**
rubbings

Materials

One or two examples of rubbings from textures in the room.
Newsprint, rice paper, or other soft but tough paper
Crayons and soft pencils
Masking tape, scissors, and glue
A large sheet of butcher paper attached to the display space
(Let the students decide on a color that will set the rubbing off well.)

Preparation

Before starting the rubbing project:

Initiate a class discussion about the textures of the materials that can be found in the room.

What **textures** do you see around you?

Can you recognize some of these textures just by looking at them?

What other sense will you need to find out about textures?

Which ones are hard? Soft? Smooth? Rough? Warm? Cold? Tight? Open?

Which textures would be the best subjects for making a **rubbing**? (Those with contrast, sharp edges, and depth of **relief**, or indentation.)

Procedure

Have a surface ready for demonstrating how to make a rubbing. Go through the process, noting each step on a chart as you do it, so the students will have a reminder of the procedure.

Explain to the students:

Rubbings are really fun to do, but they won't turn out well if you don't work very carefully and follow the instructions.

Let's go through the steps together.

Select the surface:

Remember what we discussed about textures that will make a good rubbing.

Select the paper:

Cut a piece that is quite a bit bigger than the area that you are going to rub.

Press the paper on the surface:

Go over the paper with your hands to smooth it out and stretch it firmly over the surface.

Tape it down:

Using masking tape, fasten the paper all around the edges so there is no chance of it moving. (Check the students before they start rubbing.)

Rub in one direction:

Find the direction that is comfortable, then start at the center and work out to the edges, but always in the same direction. An exception is when there is a clearly defined edge, then just the edges are worked from the inside to the outside all the way around.

Cover well:

Press firmly but not too hard and go over it until the imprint is as visible as the material and the surface will allow. Using the side of a peeled crayon works well.

Have the rubbing checked:

Check the students to be sure they have done the best job possible before allowing them to remove the tape and start another rubbing.

If they have chosen a surface that isn't too suitable for rubbing, discuss this with them and allow them to make another selection.

Rubbings can be of different sizes and a small one can be repeated several times to make a larger design.

When each student has completed several rubibngs, initiate a discussion using the different categories that were mentioned earlier (rough, smooth, etc.)

Write the categories spaced across the top of the butcher paper. Ask if there are others that should be added.

Explain to the students:

Now you are going to place your rubbings in the proper category. You may trim them if you wish.

There are some very nice rubbings here. That is because all the steps in the process were done very carefully. Now that you understand the process, you will be able to make rubbings of good quality any place you find good textures.

After the students have moved the pieces around and decided on a final display arrangement, have them fasten the rubbings down firmly. Ask them to write the names of the various materials represented in each category.

Closure

There is so much to see all around us that it often becomes confusing and we need help in sorting it all out. Doing texture rubbings is one way of doing this. It helps us focus on small details. As you look for textures to rub, you will see things that you never noticed before. You will also begin to notice what things are made of.

Let's see how this works out in the community. Each of you should take enough material for two or three rubbings. See what you can find that would make nice additions to our display. You can add categories as you find new things.

Remember to do all the steps carefully. We want examples of good quality for our display.

This could be a class activity on a walk through the neighborhood community. Making rubbings in a cemetery could be part of a history lesson.

HANGING THE SHOW

Theme

The arrangement of a group of student drawings, photographs, or magazine cut-outs offers a way to involve a whole class in making a visual statement about their community that includes aesthetics, content, and a group decision-making process.

Learning Objectives

To experience the group process for decision making
To develop ability to synthesize information using a visual media
To develop aesthetic appreciation of arrangement of objects in space

Subject Matter

Social Studies
Art
Language Arts

Time

Forty-five minutes minimum
Recommended:
Forty-five minutes for discussion and preliminary layout
Forty-five minutes for final presentation
Fifteen minutes for a class critique of the show

Vocabulary Words

critique   **creative involvement**

Materials

Student drawings or photographs of observations made in the community or cut from magazines (from previous activities)
A wall or display space in the classroom, or elsewhere in the school or in the community.
Paper or cardboard for mounting
Butcher paper for background
Tape, pens, glue, tacks, etc.

Preparation

The activity could be utilized as a follow-up for any art or visual research project, but it is recommended here as a culmination of one of the community investigations such as the sketching or texture rubbing activities.

Procedure

Explain to the students:

> When artists put up displays of their work, they call it "hanging the show." The artists give a lot of thought to the design of a show. They want their work to look its best, they want people to be interested in it and to understand the message that they are trying to communicate.

> Today we are going to hang a show of the materials that you have assembled. We want it to be attractive, to create interest and to communicate a message—that means to tell a story about the project that you have done. To do this successfully we should work out a design for the show the way the artists do.

Have the students put a piece of masking tape in their materials and hang them temporarily on a wall surface that is not the one to be used for the show, perhaps a portable blackboard.

Ask them to look carefully at all the material and then make suggestions on how they might be assembled to tell the story. Possibilities are to put them in categories by building type or details, by chronological order, or in a series as they were seen on a walk. Make suggestions, but let the students come up with the ideas.

Since the materials are loosely taped to the board, they can be easily moved around to try out various arrangements and groupings.

When they have decided on the story or message and how the materials are to be grouped, initiate a discussion on ideas for hanging the show so that it will have the greatest impact. Suggest that they give thought to:

the location:
good light
good viewing
sufficient room

the background:
existing wall surface
butcher paper in selected color
if the material should be mounted how they should be mounted
how they should be mounted

After deciding on the space and getting the background ready, they can start working on the final form of the show. Have the students place the materials, still loosely taped, in the groupings previously chosen on the permanent background. When all the materials are there to be viewed initiate a discussion that gives consideration to:

the hanging:
total effect
arrangement of the pieces
size and shape of the spaces in between
how fastened
colors
titles or word explanations

the message:
what story does it tell about the community
what kind (old, new, changing, mixed)
what condition (cared for, needing improvement)
what is special about it

Before the final fastening in place have the students **critique** the show, that is, look it over with a critical eye to see if it does what they want it to do. Make any adjustments that seem necessary.

Add words only if they are needed.

Closure

You have a very nice show here. Now let's look at what you have learned in this project. You have

utilized research materials
participated in group discussion
made group decisions
produced a visual message

This is a process for **creative involvement** in the community.

This will help you gain an understanding of how to put information together if you want to propose some change in the community or if you want to fight a change that you feel would not be for the best. Now you have a useful tool for community involvement.

SCAVENGER HUNTING IN THE COMMUNITY

Theme

Systems for making notations of what is being seen in the community are wonderful ways to increase environmental awareness and to give it meaning. If attention can be drawn to a certain series of specific subjects for observing the room, school, neighborhood, town, city center, or region, they can be experienced in much greater detail and scope of understanding.

Learning Objectives

To increase the use of the senses in observation
To experience a replicable system for gathering, recording, and organizing information

Subject Matter

Social Studies
Science
Math
Language Arts

Time

Prior to classroom session:
Thirty minutes to select the area for the hunt

In the classroom:
Fifteen minutes for classroom discussion
Thirty to forty-five minutes for the walk
Thirty minutes for discussion upon return

Vocabulary Words

resource   **record**

Materials

Copies for each student of the sheet, "Scavenger Hunting in the Community"
Clip or cake boards
Paper and pencils or pens
1 or 2 pocket pencil sharpeners

Preparation

Before the classroom session:

Select an area for the scavenger hunt and walk through it, noting interesting details. It should be a relatively small area—the equivalent of three or four blocks should be enough. This will allow more concentration on details.

Reproduce the example of the hand-out sheet illustrated here or develop a similar one of your own. Another way would be to break each subject into a separate task card and let the students choose one.

Contract an appropriate number of adults to assist with this activity. Give them copies of the whole lesson plan to read through. Explain that they are to be a resource to the students. Students should go out in pairs or small groups.

You might want to decide on a prize or a special privilege for those who find the most items.

Procedure

Before going on the scavenger hunt:
Initiate a class discussion:

> Have you ever been on a scavenger hunt?
>
> What did you look for?
>
> Did you just look or did you bring things back with you?
>
> Today we are going on a scavenger hunt but you are not going to bring back any objects. Instead you will bring back a **record** of what you have seen. It takes concentration to really see a lot of things around you. You will probably see a lot of things that aren't on the list. Having too much to see often makes it so confusing that we stop looking. Focusing on a few details helps us see and understand an environment better. Let's see who can concentrate the hardest and find the most things on the hunt.

Hand out the sheet, "Scavenger Hunting in the Community."

> You will be filling in this sheet with the things you will find. You should try to have at least one example of each thing. Some of them may not be in your area. However, you should be able to find several examples of others.

Go over the sheet to see if there are questions. If you have decided on a prize . . .

> There will be something special (tell them what it is or make it a surprise) for the three of you who have found the most items on your scavenger hunt.

The adult with your group will be a **resource** person to help you see as many things as possible. They will not tell you where things are but will let you know they are there to be seen.

While on the walk keep pointing things out that relate to the sheet and encourage the students to report what they are seeing to you. Question them about what they are seeing. This gets them started and broadens the scope for all of them.

Upon returning to the classroom:

Ask the students to report their findings in a general discussion. Determine who has found the most and make the awards. This provides further discussion of the things they have seen and is a way to keep them involved.

Closure

One of the problems in our society is getting people to care about the environment in which they live, work, or play. Because there are more and more people and they are using up more and more of our space and resources, it is very important that we all take responsibility for the conservation and wise use of those resources. One of the first steps is to become aware of how these resources are being used and for what purpose. On your way home today see if you can find some more things to add to your sheet. Bring it back in the morning and we will talk about it again.

SCAVENGER HUNTING

THIS IS A CHART TO HELP YOU SEE MORE WHEN YOU LOOK. WHEN YOU HAVE FOUND SOMETHING ON YOUR HUNT, WRITE IN WHERE IT WAS FOUND AND CHECK OFF THE PROPER BLANK.

CATAGORY	LOCATION WHERE?	SPECIFIC DETAILS					
BUILDING MATERIALS		CONCRETE	BRICK	WOOD	GLASS	METAL	OTHER
HOUSES							
GARDENS							
SCHOOLS							
STORES							
OFFICE BUILDINGS							
PARK OR PLAYGROUND							
OTHER							
BUILDING TYPES		HOUSE	MULTIPLE DWELLING	STORES & SHOPS	OFFICES	RESTAURANT	OTHER
1 STORY							
2 STORY							
3 STORY							
OTHER							
LAND USE		SPECIAL PLANTING	PLAY EQUIPMENT	MACHINES	SHELTERS	SPECIAL FEATURES	OTHER
GARDEN							
CONSTRUCTION AREA							
RECREATION AREA							
OTHER							

INTERVIEWING COMMUNITY RESIDENTS

Theme

Often what is perceived by sensory observation is not enough to fully understand the character of a community. Interviewing residents or workers can add another dimension to the research.

Learning Objectives

To gain an ability to conduct an interview and to record information
To organize recorded information
To utilize information to develop conclusions

Subject Matter

Social Studies
Math
Science
Language Arts

Time

Prior to the classroom session:
Thirty minutes to select the area for interviews

In the classroom:
Thirty minutes for classroom preparation
Thirty to forty-five minutes for the walk
Twenty to thirty minutes for follow-up discussion

Vocabulary Words
community   **character**
interview

Materials

Hand-out sheet, "Learning About the Environment by Interviewing"—enough copies for each student
Clip or cake boards
Pencils or pens
1 or 2 pocket pencil sharpeners

Preparation

Before the interview session:

Select the area where the interviews are to be conducted. It would be best if the area had considerable foot traffic so students can interview people on the street. If they are going to knock on doors, it should be an area where some of the students live.

Contact an appropriate number of adults to assist with this activity. Give them copies of the lesson plan to read thoroughly. They are to be a resource to the students.

If this is being done as an extension of the Sketching in the Community activity, the area where the sketches were made should be included.

An interview sheet could be prepared to fit your specific situation or use the example illustrated here.

Procedure

One way of finding out a great deal about a **community** is to find out what different people think about it. An older person will have different feelings than a younger one. A resident of a community will have different feelings than a younger one. A resident of a community will have different information than a visitor. A person who has lived in a community a long time will have different ideas than a newer resident. Each of these people has an important contribution to make. One answer can be just as good as another. **Interviewing** many people and considering the answers can give a broad picture of the **character** of a community.

Tell the students that they will be going out in pairs. One will ask the questions and the other will record the answers. Each pair is to interview two people. They will take turns so that each person has the experience of asking the questions and each has the opportunity to fill out their interview form.

Go over the interview form so that all the students are familiar with and understand the questions.

Adult assistants should listen to the discussion.

Initiate a discussion about conducting the interview.

What should you do first when you walk up to someone? (Introduce themselves—how?)

What else will people want to know about what you are doing? (Tell about the project and why it is being done.)

What will you do if someone doesn't have time to talk to you? (Be polite anyway.)

What if they want to talk to you about something else? (Keep to the questions.)

Let's practice a little before we go out.

Have the students number off by twos and then practice conducting the interview on each other. You might want to have one pair give a demonstration in front of the class and then have the class make suggestions for improving the interview technique.

While students are doing the interviewing, adults should see that they are keeping to the task, staying within the selected area, and are aware of the time schedule.

Upon returning to the classroom:

Have the students report their answers to the questions and list them on a wall chart similar to the illustration.

When all the answers to the questions are recorded, initiate a class discussion about what the information might tell us about the community.

As a result of the discussion have the students develop five statements about the character of the community and write them on the chart.

Closure

There are many ways to learn about a community. Most of them can be done by looking and recording what is seen in some way. However, there may be things that we can't see and that are important to know, if we are to really understand and evaluate a community situation. The opinions of one or two people probably wouldn't be enough to get a good picture, but interviewing a number of people gives us a lot of input from which we can develop conclusions. Take your sheets home tonight and conduct the interview on someone there. Bring it back tomorrow and we will discuss your answers and see if your statements still seem all right or if we want to change them.

LEARNING ABOUT THE COMMUNITY BY INTERVIEWING

INTERVIEWER'S NAME

SCHOOL

1. HOW LONG HAVE YOU LIVED IN THIS COMMUNITY?_____

2. WHERE DID YOU LIVE BEFORE YOU MOVED HERE?_____

3. HOW LONG DO YOU THINK MOST PEOPLE HAVE LIVED HERE? 1 YEAR___ 5 YEARS___ 10 YEARS___ MORE___

4. HOW MANY PEOPLE DO YOU KNOW IN THIS COMMUNITY? NONE_____ FEW_____ MANY_____

5. DO YOU RECOGNIZE MOST OF THE PEOPLE THAT LIVE AROUND HERE EVEN THOUGH YOU DON'T KNOW THEM?_____

6. DOES THE COMMUNITY PLAN PARTIES OR PROJECTS TOGETHER?_____

7. IF THERE WAS TROUBLE WOULD PEOPLE HELP EACH OTHER?_____

8. WHAT IS THE BEST FEATURE OF THE COMMUNITY?_____

9. WHAT WOULD YOU MOST LIKE TO SEE CHANGED?_____
    _____

10. OTHER COMMENTS:_____
    _____

CHART FOR RECORDING INTERVIEW RESPONSES

1	2	3	4	5	6	7	8
TOTALS							

SAMPLE SUMMARY

BASED ON THIS INFORMATION THE FOLLOWING STATEMENTS CAN BE MADE ABOUT THIS COMMUNITY:

1. IT IS A MIXTURE OF OLD AND NEW RESIDENTS.
2. MOST PEOPLE COME FROM THE MID-WEST.
3. PEOPLE RECOGNIZE BUT DON'T KNOW OTHER RESIDENTS.
4. THE PARK IS AN IMPORTANT FEATURE.
5. PEOPLE DON'T WANT IT TO CHANGE.

5 PEOPLE SPACES

INTRODUCTION

Theme

Everyone is occupying space or moving through it in all living moments. Each person is also causing an effect on the space, as well as being affected by it. Research has shown that there are quite predictable spatial relationships that can cause, prevent, or alter the activities that occur in a space.

Knowing something about these relationships increases knowledge and understanding of the people spaces in our environment.

The Activities

1. Here's How to Get to My Place
2. Facts, Figures, and Feelings
3. How Much Room Do You Need?
4. Where Do the Bubbles Go?
5. School Spaces

These activities involve the student in mapping, surveying, measuring, and manipulating the spaces that are most familiar to them, the home and the school.

Curriculum Areas

Math and Science through measuring, mapping, working in scale, and comparing figures
through utilizing a scientific process for doing research

Social Studies through group participation, cooperation, and production of a visual example
through understanding of the effect of spatial relationships on human behavior
through gaining in the ability to communicate by conducting surveys and presenting results

Language Arts through new vocabulary, recording answers, and group discussion

Art through working with color, symbol keys, and spatial arrangements

Where

The activities are done partially in the classroom and partially on field investigations.

Why

Each of the methods—mapping, surveying, measuring, and plan drawing—demonstrate effective processes for increasing environmental awareness. The process also illustrates efficient, as well as attractive, ways of putting information into a communicable visual form.

Extensions

The activities may be used separately or as part of some other group of exercises. The processes have many applications.

If the whole group of activities is done, the culmination might be a display or presentation of all that has been learned about the area and the school.

All the information could be used to make a decision about some kind of environmental change that students could implement.

Bibliography

Mapping Small Places by L. F. Wentworth, et al, Winston Press, Minneapolis, 1972.

Many practical suggestions for mapping techniques and exercises.

Hidden Dimension by Edward T. Hall, Doubleday, New York, 1969.

The spatial bubble concept is described in detail. There is also interesting information on animal territoriality.

Personal Space: The Behavioral Basis of Design by Robert Sommer, Prentice Hall, Englewood Cliffs, N.J., 1969.

More ideas about human behavior in relation to space.

Defensible Space by Oscar Newman, Macmillan, New York, 1972.

The effects of the arrangement of spaces on such things as vandalism, protection and the development of a sense of community.

HERE'S HOW TO GET TO MY PLACE

Theme

Reading a map in order to find your way around a new place or drawing one to give directions to another person are skills that are often needed but with which even many adults have had little experience.

Learning Objectives

To understand some basic elements that increase map reading ability
To develop an ability to visually record an experience
To gain an understanding of scale and distance

Subject Matter

Social Studies
Math/Science
Art

Time

One or two 45- to 60-minute classroom sessions
One or two days for the assignment
One-half hour in classroom for closure

Vocabulary Words

pace	**proportion**
scale	**symbol key**

Materials

18″ × 24″ sheets of white paper or pieces of butcher paper or newsprint
Pencils and pens
Several maps

Preparation

Students will have established their average pace previously (See page 180 of Useful Tools.)

Procedure

Introduction to the students:

> If you are going to become good environmental investigators, you need to practice some techniques that you will use over and over again and in different ways.

> When you want to go to a strange place or you are lost and beginning to get a little scared, what do you wish you had? (A map.) If you want to tell someone how to get some place, why is a map better than just giving them the directions? Yes, when you tell something to another person, they may not see the same picture in their minds that you have in yours. They also may not be listening carefully enough or may forget some very important piece of information. So drawing a picture of the directions—a map—will make it much easier.

> Today you are going to draw a map that will tell someone who has never been there how to get from the school to the place where you live.

> (This portion is optional.) You will measure the distances by using the **pace** you have established earlier. If you take the bus or someone drives you, you can pace the portions that you walk. How can you find out the distances that you drive? (Check the speedometer when you start and when you get out.)

> However, even if you give someone a well drawn map, they still may get lost. Can you think why that might be? When they go out the front door of the school, which way are they going to turn? If they turn the wrong way, they will never get to your place, will they? How can we get them started in the right direction? What do you usually find on a map that indicates direction? (A north arrow.) Yes, and you will notice that the north arrow points to the top of the paper. Map makers agreed a long time ago that it would be helpful if all the maps were drawn the same way. Of course, you may always find someone who wants to be different, but you can usually depend on north being at the top of your map. That is quite a comfort if you are lost and are trying to find your way home.

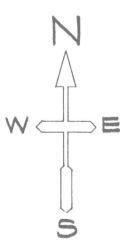

Draw a north arrow on a chart in the proper relation to the front door of the school. Adding the other three directions to the arrow will help the students in establishing the direction of their route home.

> Look at our directional arrow and decide which way you go home. Remember we are all starting at the same place—the front door of the school.

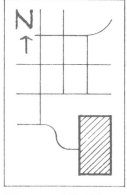

FIGURE 1

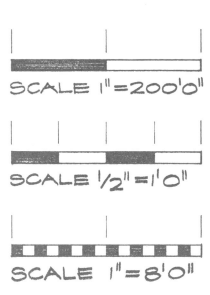

FIGURE 2

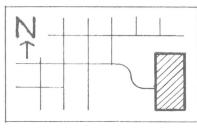

SCALE 1" = 200'0"

SCALE 1/2" = 1'0"

SCALE 1" = 8'0"

Now think about where you are going to locate the school on your drawing. Will you all put it in the same place on the paper? Do you all go home in the same direction away from the school? You will want to place the school on the paper so that you leave enough room for the rest of your map. If you go north from the door of the school, your drawing should look like this (Figure 1). If you go west of the school, your drawing should look like this (Figure 2).

Draw the figures as you talk or have them on the chart beforehand.

Before you draw the school on your sheet, there is still one other thing that you need to think about. How big are you going to draw it? Besides the north arrow, there is always something else on a map. Have you ever noticed what it is? Yes. There will be an indication of what the **scale** is. The scale is what tells you how big the area is that the map covers. On the same size sheet of paper you may have a map of a very large area at a rather small scale or you may have a map of a small area at a rather large scale.

Show examples of maps at two distinct scales.

The indication of the scale will look something like this. (Show the scale on the map and draw the example.) It might say 1" = 200', or 1" = 8'. There are many different scales. The scale selected will depend on how big the area is that is to be drawn on the sheet. We won't use an actual measurement for our scale on this map but you will need to think about how big the area is that you will be drawing in **proportion** to the size of the sheet of paper you are using.

If you live quite close to the school, you won't have as much information to put on your sheet, will you? What does that tell you about the size of your drawing? Will it be large or small? Yes, it can be a fairly large drawing.

If you live a longer distance away from the school, how will you draw the school? Right. You will draw it smaller so you can get all the streets and roads on your map. Indicate the comparative sizes of the drawings of the school on Figures 1 and 2.

Maps have lots information on them. Besides the north arrow and the scale, what else is often there? Yes, a **symbol key** that tells you how things are being shown on the map. It will help you in drawing your map if you work out a key ahead of time. The key usually is

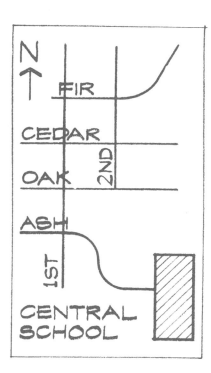

drawn in the corner so that it doesn't interfere with the map itself. Start your key with a symbol for the school. It might be a rectangle, a school bell, a flag—whatever you like. It can be any thing as long as you explain it in the key.

Now you are ready to start your map. You have three things to put on it; the north arrow, the scale, and the symbol key. First decide on the location of the school or the drawing in relation to where you will draw your route home. Work in pencil until you are sure that you have it in the right place. You should draw your whole map in pencil so that you can make changes. Later you can decide on a nice color scheme and go over it with colored pens. Along with deciding on the location of the school, you must decide on how big to draw it.

Go around helping them with these decisions.

Now draw an arrow that indicates where the front door of the school is located. Where is the front door in relation to north? Put the north arrow on your map near the edge of the paper. Map makers like to make their north arrows look very fancy. Design a nice north arrow. Now where is the top of your map? (Where the north arrow points.) Your map should be read with the paper facing in the north direction, shouldn't it? If you want your map to be easily used, how will you place the paper on your desk when you are writing in the notes and street names? Right. It will help the person who uses it if it can be held in the north position and the information can be read without having to turn it all around.

When the students have this information recorded on their maps, they are ready for the assignment.

In the next day or two you are to complete your maps from the school to your place. This means you will need to be making careful observations as you go back and forth to school. It would be a good idea to make some notes. You will need to add more symbols for such things as houses, intersections, stop signs or lights, and landmarks—the special things that always tell you where you are. Of course, you can't put everything on your map. That would make it too confusing. Put only as much as you think another person will need to follow it.

Knowing the distances is important too. The person needs to know if it is a long way to go or if it is close by. You can observe comparative distances or you can measure by counting the paces between the things you show on your map, such as between one intersection and another. Just write it in the number of paces as you go along. You can convert them into feet and inches when you get back to school. If you are driving, record the speedometer reading when you start and when you get out. That can be converted to miles when you get back to school and added to the distances that you paced while walking before and after riding.

Map makers have been very important people in our history. Let's see what kind of map makers you can be.

Closure

Display the completed maps and have the class discuss their experiences making the maps. In looking them over ask them to comment on the things that make them the most clear and easy to follow.

Good maps are those that give all the necessary information but that don't try to tell you too much. The design of the symbol key is very important in making a map readable. Neat and accurate drawings in nice colors make the maps attractive as well as useful.

Maps are fascinating to study. They give lots of information about a place. They can help you imagine what it might be like to be there. Old ones can be compared with new ones and tell you a lot about the history. One place can be compared with another. You can see the similarities between the place where you live and other places. Look over these maps and let's see what information we can find.

Have maps of larger cities and small towns and old and new maps for the students to study. This could also be used as an opportunity to study maps in the social studies book more thoroughly.

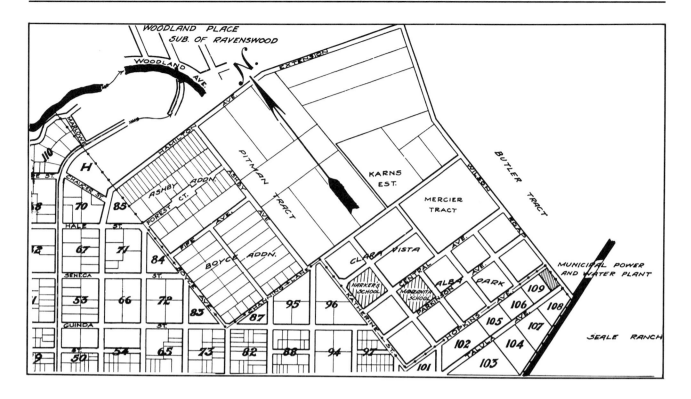

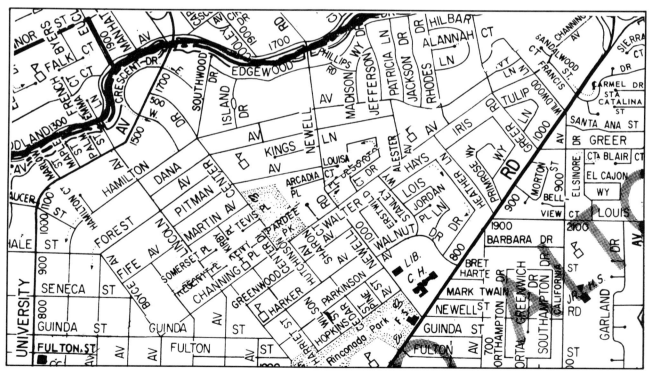

A portion of a map of Palo Alto, California, in 1920 (top) and in 1980. You may want to reproduce the page and ask students to comment on how the area has changed in 60 years. As a starting point, have them look to the northeast from the intersection of Boyce and Channing.

FACTS, FIGURES, AND FEELINGS

Theme

Developing an effective package to create or prevent environmental change requires good visual materials supported by factual research. The school environment can be a good learning laboratory for trying out a variety of investigative techniques. Conducting a survey is one useful technique.

Learning Objectives

To learn how to conduct a survey
To gain ability in gathering and recording information
To increase the ability to observe the environment

Subject Matter

Social Studies
Language Arts
Math

Time

One 45- to 60-minute classroom period for the interview portion
One 45- to 60-minute classroom period for evaluating, collating, and discussing the results of the survey

Vocabulary Words

survey   **collating**
record

Materials

Copies of Sheets 1, 2, and 3 for the members of each group. Each member of a group should have a copy of the survey sheet for their group. A few extras would be a good idea, especially of Sheet 3.
Pencils/pens

Procedure

Inform the whole school staff about the survey activity the students will be doing.
   The students could develop their own surveys, particularly if

you have some special goal in mind. If not, these examples illustrated here will work quite well. They provide a system for focusing on an environment and information for moving on to some other project relating to the school.

How long have you been going to this school? How many are new this year? How many are in their second year? How many have been here for three or four years? Have any of you been here since you started school?

Well, some of you have been here quite awhile. (Revise if yours is a new school.) Do you know when the school was built? Who built it? Where it got its name?

Since you spend a lot of time here those should be things that you would like to know. There are a lot more things like that that would be interesting to know if you just happened to think of them. That is the problem we have about looking at the environments that we live in, go to school in, or play or shop in. We don't give them enough thought to find out some of the interesting things about them. What would be a technique that would help you find out more interesting things about an environment?

Press for answers such as:
asking people
looking it up in a library
a survey

Asking people questions is a good way of finding out a lot of things. If you are going to put this information to use you need a way to **record** it. Having a **survey** form with questions and spaces for answers is a very efficient way to record information and to get information from many people. The survey sheet allows you to ask questions and get opinions on the same questions of a number of different people, to record the answers, and to make totals of figures and facts or to compare feelings.

You are going to conduct a survey of the school. You will use three different survey sheets. Each one is planned to get a specific kind of information. When you have finished the surveys, all the information will be put together. That is called **collating** the information. The result should give a very good verbal picture of the school.

Surveys can be designed for many different purposes but these particular three surveys are planned to learn facts, figures, and feelings about the school. The class will work in three groups to gather this information, one group for each type of survey. Each person will fill out a survey sheet.

Assign the students to Group 1.

Give a copy of Sheet 1 to a student who will be a good group leader or have the group choose one.

Would you read the questions on this survey sheet to the class?

Who do you think will have this information? Yes, there could be records in the library and the district administrative office keeps records, but probably the first thing to do would be to talk to the principal. You don't want to take too much of his or her time so it would be a good idea for the group to work together on this.

Make an appointment for the group to meet with the principal. Decide on which questions each will ask (everyone should participate). All members of the group will fill in their survey sheets completely, not just the answers to the questions they ask. Remember that you are finding out facts. Your answers must be the facts you have been told and must be recorded correctly. Your answers cannot be your opinions.

Be sure and thank the principal for the time. Compare your answers afterward and choose a person who prints well to fill in the information that the group has agreed is correct on a sheet to turn in.

Hand out surveys to Group 1.

Assign the students in Group 2.

Give a copy of Sheet 2 to another student who will be a good group leader or have the group choose one.

Would you read the questions on this survey sheet to the class?

As you have heard, this survey deals with figures—the number of rooms and the number of people in the school. Who do you think will have this information? Perhaps you will have to get it from a number of people so it will be a good idea to assign people in your group different parts of the survey to conduct.

You could get the information about the rooms in the school yourself, by observation. If there are a few locked doors, you will have to ask someone about those. At least two people should be working together so they can compare and check their sheets to be sure they haven't duplicated or forgotten anything.

The school secretary would be able to give you figures

on the numbers of students. The custodian and the principal would be able to give you information on the school services and on those who use the building.

Decide which group members will do each thing. Have each of the group members fill out their assigned portion so they can check each other. Remember you must get correct answers from someone who knows. Don't make any guesses!

When you have all the information, choose a person who prints nicely to fill in a clean sheet with answers the group has agreed on to hand in.

Hand out survey sheets to Group 2.
 Assign the students to Group 3.
 Give a copy of Sheet 3 to a student who will be a good group leader or have the group choose one.

Read the questions on this survey sheet to the class.

This survey deals with feelings about the school. What is different about it from the other two? The others dealt with facts and figures and for those things there is only one correct answer. This survey deals with how people feel about the school environment. How one person feels is just as correct as another person's feeling. How will that affect how we conduct this part of the survey? Can you survey only one or two people? Everyone has feelings about the school, so you will need to survey several people who represent different points of view. Who do you think they should be?

Press for answers such as . . .
a classroom teacher or two
a special teacher (gym, music, etc.)
a young student
an older student
a parent
a custodian
a secretary
an administrator

Your group will conduct several different surveys. You won't be comparing your answers to see if they are correct. There are no right or wrong answers about feelings. You will be comparing your surveys to see what the differences and similarities in the feelings are.

It is easier to work with someone else when surveying, so divide in groups of two. One person can ask the questions and the other record the answers. Each pair should talk to at least two people so each person will have the opportunity to both question and record.

The whole group should decide which people each pair will contact. Since everyone can feel just as they wish and all their answers are right, the group will have to make up a sheet listing all the different answers to each question and share it with the class.

Hand out survey sheets to Group 3.

As all the groups go out to conduct their surveys there are a couple of things that you should all remember. Introduce yourself and tell the person you are talking to just what you are doing. Be polite and businesslike so you don't take up too much of their time. Always thank them for helping you.

When all the surveys are completed and the final sheets posted, ask each group to share their information with the whole class and initiate a discussion about what all this information tells them about their school. Press for comments on such things as . . .
history
size
use by other groups
what would you want to change
what do you want to stay the same

Closure

Your surveys have turned up a lot of information. You know a good deal more about your school than you did before you conducted your surveys.

Knowing some facts about anything increases your interest in it. The more you know about something, usually the more you want to know. Finding out how people feel about a place, especially if those feelings turn out to be different from your own, can help you see things that you hadn't thought of before.

Surveys provide a good system for getting and recording information and for expanding your awareness of an environment.

FACTS, FIGURES, AND FEELINGS
SURVEY SHEET 1: FACTS

1. WHEN WAS THE SCHOOL BUILT?_____

2. HOW MUCH DID IT COST?

   _____

3. WHO DESIGNED THE SCHOOL?
   _____ (ARCHITECT)

4. WHO BUILT THE SCHOOL?
   _____ (CONTRACTOR)

5. HAVE THERE BEEN ADDITIONS TO THE
   SCHOOL? WHEN?_____

6. WHO DESIGNED THE ADDITIONS?
   _____ (ARCHITECT)

7. WHO BUILT THE ADDITIONS?
   _____ (CONTRACTOR)

8. ARE THERE ADDITIONS TO THE SCHOOL
   PLANNED?_____

9. WHERE DID THE STUDENTS GO BEFORE
   THIS SCHOOL WAS BUILT?

   _____

10. ARE THERE ANY CHANGES PLANNED
    RELATING TO THE STUDENTS WHO
    ATTEND THIS SCHOOL?_____

11. WHAT BUILDING MATERIALS HAVE BEEN
    USED IN THIS SCHOOL?
    INSIDE?   _____

    _____

    _____

    _____

    OUTSIDE?_____

    _____

    _____

    _____

FACTS, FIGURES, AND FEELINGS
SURVEY SHEET 2 : FIGURES

1. THE NUMBER OF ROOMS FOR EACH OF THE FOLLOWING:

    KINDERGARTEN   _____
    FIRST GRADE   _____
    SECOND GRADE   _____
    THIRD GRADE   _____
    FOURTH GRADE   _____
    FIFTH GRADE   _____
    SIXTH GRADE   _____
    OTHERS   _____
    REST ROOMS - GIRLS   _____
                    BOYS   _____
    STORAGE AND CLOSETS _____
    SPECIAL ROOMS   _____

    TOTAL NUMBER OF ROOMS_____

2. THE NUMBER OF PEOPLE FOR EACH OF THE FOLLOWING:

    KINDERGARTEN   _____
    FIRST GRADE   _____
    SECOND GRADE   _____
    THIRD GRADE   _____
    FOURTH GRADE   _____
    FIFTH GRADE   _____
    SIXTH GRADE   _____
    OTHERS   _____
    STAFF: TEACHERS   _____
          OFFICE   _____
          SPECIAL   _____
          CUSTODIAL   _____

    TOTAL NUMBER OF STAFF _____

FACTS, FIGURES, AND FEELINGS
SURVEY SHEET 3 : FEELINGS

1. WHAT DO YOU LIKE BEST ABOUT THIS SCHOOL ?_____

2. WHAT DO YOU LIKE LEAST ABOUT THIS SCHOOL ?_____

3. IS IT EASY OR HARD TO FIND YOUR WAY AROUND ?_____

4. WHAT WOULD MAKE IT EASIER FOR STRANGERS ?_____

5. COULD THE SCHOOL BUILDING BE USED MORE ?_____ BY WHOM ?_____

6. IS THE SCHOOL BUILDING TOO LARGE ? _____ TOO SMALL ?_____

7. IS THE SCHOOL YARD TOO LARGE ?_____ TOO SMALL ?_____

8. WHICH AREAS OR ROOM IN THE SCHOOL ARE USED THE MOST ?_____ THE LEAST ?_____

9. WHICH AREAS OR ROOMS DO YOU LIKE BEST IN RELATION TO:

   COLOR_____

   LIGHT_____

   EQUIPMENT_____

   SIZE_____

   SOUND_____

   SMELLS_____

   TASTES_____

   FURNITURE_____

   WHAT OTHER THINGS ?_____

10. IF YOU COULD DO ANYTHING YOU WISH TO THE SCHOOL WHAT WOULD YOU DO ?_____

HOW MUCH ROOM DO YOU NEED?

Theme

Everyone is occupying a space at all times. Learning about the spaces we keep to ourselves and those we share with others and how various types of behavior can occur because of the arrangement of the space itself can increase environmental awareness. Such a study can be used as a tool for developing a sense of community and cooperation.

Learning Objectives

To understand ways in which space is used
To gain vocabulary and understanding relating to some abstract concepts concerning space
To learn some spatial concepts through measured distance, movement, and sensory awareness

Subject Matter

Social Studies
Math
Language Arts

Time

Teacher: One half hour to go through the lesson plan to establish timing and emphasis
Students: Forty-five minutes to one hour

Vocabulary Words

space   **space bubble**   **visualize**

Materials

Pencils
Rulers
Masking tape

Procedure

Introduction to the students:

> When you hear the words *outer space* you have a
> pretty good picture in your mind of what you think that

space looks like. However, you have probably never thought much about how the space that *you* take up all the time, wherever you are, actually looks. Each of us is always occupying some space. If two of you try to take up the same space, you may get in a fight over it. If your space is too far away from your friend's space you will not be able to talk to each other, so you will probably move your spaces closer together. Today we are going to have a little fun experiencing different spaces. This will help us become aware of how different distances in the spaces around us have something to do with how we feel about the other people in those spaces.

Give the instructions slowly so the students will have enough time between each comment to allow their thinking to be stretched as far as their capabilities will allow. The students may want to laugh at some of the instructions. Remind them that they are not to comment out loud or make any sounds. This is a "mind trip"—a thinking experience. Repeat the reminder if necessary. Closed eyes help!

Ask the students to stand up and spread out so they have quite a little space around them.

With your arms at your sides, look all around yourself without moving out of place. Look up. Look down. Look to one side and then the other.

Now close your eyes. Keep them closed tight until you are told to open them. This will make it easier for you to sense the space sense the noises in the room. Think about the floor on which you are standing. Let your body feel very light on the floor. Now let yourself feel very heavy on the floor. Be aware of the others somewhere around you.

With your eyes still closed, think about the room you are in. Focus your thoughts on the door, the windows, the desks, the ceiling. How do you enter the room? How do you go to your desk? Where is the teacher? What place in the room do you like the best?

Open your eyes and look around. Does the room really look the way you **visualized** it?

Close your eyes again. Now stretch your arms out and revolve slowly. Think about the larger space that you *now* occupy. Do you sense that you might collide with someone else? Can you sense other people's arms near you? Think about how you feel about those other arms. Are they taking up some of your space? Are you bothered by them being there? Maybe you are irritated? Do you feel that you want to defend your space? Do you want to keep it for yourself?

Open your eyes and say "hi" to a person near you. Now do you have a different feeling about them? Does it feel as if your own space has become a little bigger? Would you like to invite the person to share your space or would you rather keep it just for yourself?

Ask the students to sit down on the floor and give them this information.

Do you know that we all live in our own little **space bubble?** Studies have shown that people have some quite definite and similar ideas about their personal space bubble in relation to themselves and to the space that is just outside this bubble. The studies tell us that the size of everyone's space bubble is about 18 inches out from your skin in all directions. Take your ruler and stretch your arm out to the side. Measure out 18 inches from your shoulder and place a piece of masking tape on your arm at that point. You may need to help each other with this. Now turn around while standing in the same place and watch the mark on your arm. Think of yourself enclosed in a plastic bubble that is the size indicated by that 18-inch mark. This is your very personal space that you keep for your family and close friends to share with you. It is where kissing, hugging, comforting, and protection take place. If someone started to attack you, what would you probably do? Right. You would look for someone to help you and you would get very close to them. You would want them in your personal space. In other words, they would become your close friend in a hurry!

The size of your personal space bubble can vary depending on the position your body is in. Crouch down and make your bubble as small as possible. Now your bubble is smaller and in a different position in space. Does this make the rest of the room seem different? How does it feel when I am standing over you? Do you feel little, over-powered, insignificant? Has your feeling toward the other people in the room changed? Stretch out on the floor. Now your personal bubble is horizontal instead of vertical. Are you more comfortable? Are you having trouble finding room for your bubble?

Now stand up and move toward the person next to you. Is there a point where you feel silly? Do you feel that you want to back away? Maybe you want to say "Hey, you're in *my* space!"

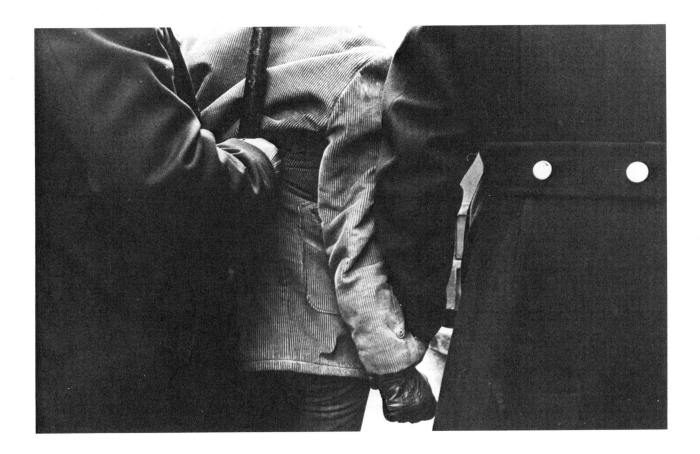

Stepping into someone's personal space bubble without being invited can cause strong reactions. It can be very threatening sometimes. You are apt to get slapped or shoved away. Getting very close to a suspect is a technique the police use for breaking them down. No one can stand having their personal space bubble invaded for very long.

Now, let's imagine a little larger bubble around us. It is called our "friendly bubble." This is the space around us for friends and personal activity. It is the space that starts at the edge of our personal space bubble—about 18 inches out from our skins—and extends out about four feet in all directions. This is about three feet beyond the end of our arms when they are stretched out. Help each other by holding a yardstick straight out from the end of your out-stretched arm. Observe carefully how far out that is.

Now turn around in place with your arms stretched out. Focus your eyes three feet beyond your arms end and notice the circle that your arms make.

Put your hands over your head and see how far up the circle goes. Imagine the same distance below your feet: the bubbles have basements, too! Now you have an idea how the space that your friendly bubble takes up looks.

Do our bubbles always stay in one place? Not very often, do they? So move around the room with your arms stretched out and notice how much room your friendly bubble is taking. Are you bumping into others? Are you retreating into a corner? Do you feel as if you want to stand your ground and defend your bubble? Do you feel kind of alone? Would you like to ask someone to share your bubble?

If you asked someone to share your friendly bubble, who would it probably be? Probably a close friend, wouldn't it? So what has happened to your bubble? Is your friend sitting close to you? Your friend may have moved into your personal space bubble. (Demonstrate.)

Ask the students to return to their desks. Have the five spatial bubble designations listed on the board.

There are five space bubbles:

personal—skin to 18 inches
friendly—18 inches to 4 feet
social—4 feet to 7 feet
casual—7 feet to 12 feet
public—12 feet to 25 feet

We have been experiencing the personal bubble and the friendly bubble. There are three more space bubbles that experts have been able to measure. One is the "social bubble," which is the space from four feet to seven feet out from your skin.

Ask one of the students to stand in an open space. Position other students around at four, five, six, and seven feet out. Use them to illustrate the size of the spaces discussed in these comments.

The social bubble includes the spaces where group activities occur. In group activities we may be quite close to each other but we are not talking with individuals. We are talking as part of a whole group. If you start talking personally to your friend you will turn or move away from the group a little. Then what are you doing? (Moving into your friendly bubble.)

The social bubble is the space for group discussions, for working together on class projects, or for working in special learning groups. Actually, all of our classroom work is done in a series of social bubbles. You often get in trouble when you talk during work time, don't you? You are changing to the friendly or the personal bubbles, aren't you?

Where does the teacher's desk fit into this bubble system? Is it always in the same bubble? (Keep posing questions to stimulate thinking about the spatial relationships.) When is it in the social bubble? (During general classroom work.) If you are talking to the teacher from the opposite side of the desk, which bubble are you in? (Friendly.) If you are showing the teachers a paper and asking for help, where would you probably stand? (Next to the teacher.) Which bubble are you in? (Personal.) If the teacher orders you to stand close by because you are to be disciplined, what is happening? Right. Your personal bubble has been invaded. You and the teacher are actually in each other's personal bubbles but you didn't have any choice and it makes you feel very uncomfortable, doesn't it?

If some work has been assigned, you will probably get down to work very quickly if the teacher moves into your social bubble. If another student is standing in your bubble looking at you, you will find it very hard to concentrate. If they are doing their own work, then you do not feel your bubble is being invaded.

If you are taking a test and the teacher stands in your social bubble, you will feel quite nervous. However, if you are enjoying drawing a picture, you may be glad to have the chance to share it. How we feel about the thing that we are doing makes a difference about how we feel about our bubbles.

If you are taking a test and the teacher is outside your social bubble, you will not be bothered. The space beyond seven feet and up to twelve feet is called your "casual bubble." This is the area where you may say hello to someone, but you don't have to. In the hallway, for instance, you might give someone you know a friendly punch as you pass or you might not acknowledge a person at all.

The largest distance in space in which people can communicate with one another is called the "public bubble." This is the distance from 12 feet to 25 feet out from your skin. It is the distance for lectures, church services, assemblies, library supervision, or giving group instructions. Using a microphone can extend this distance but those beyond the 25 feet will have difficulty relating to the person who is speaking. They will be relating to the voice and will probably have trouble concentrating on what is being said.

It is pretty easy to understand the bubbles if you think just about your home and the school. However, have you ever thought about why you sometimes get into conversations that you would rather not have while riding a bus, waiting in line, or sitting in a theater? Or maybe you have started a conversation and found a person to be quite unfriendly. Now that you know a little about bubbles, what would you say is happening here? Right. The circumstance has put you in someone's personal or friendly bubble but you don't know them. This may make you feel as if you need to talk to them or feel that you have been invaded if they talk to you. On the other hand, because you have been placed in this space, it may be the beginning of a nice friendship.

If we become aware of how we feel about our own different bubbles, how will that help us get along better with our family? With our friends? With strangers?

Try out your knowledge. Walk up very close to someone who isn't a very close friend and see if that person moves back out of the personal bubble. Ask someone you know very well a personal question from the social bubble distance and see if he or she moves toward you to give the answer. At the time when the person is not busy, move very near someone close to you. See if you don't get a hug or at least a "hi." You might even get a kiss! If you don't want one, move out of the personal bubble.

Closure

When things in outer space are discussed or you hear about a space ship going to the moon, you often hear references to millions of miles or light years away from the earth. It is all so vast that it is hard to **visualize** but, when distances from something familiar are given, it gives us some base for understanding.

A bubble in space that can't be seen is also hard to visualize, but when each bubble can be measured in relation to a person's body, it becomes easier. By measuring the various distances and observing where they are in relation to the body, the bubble takes shape, like big soap bubbles of different sizes. Observing what people do and how they react in these different-sized bubbles can be fun as well as making a contribution to your awareness of your environment.

WHERE DO THE BUBBLES GO?

Theme

A great deal of research has been done on observing people and their reactions in various spatial situations. It has been found that we all have bubbles of various sizes around us. The sizes vary according to the type of activity being done. The bubbles are imaginary but what happens within each of them is not. Certain activities work best within certain spaces. When this is understood, a much better job of planning a room or a building for the people who will use it can be done.

Learning Objectives

To conceptualize spatial dimensions
To understand relative measurement and scale
To apply spatial concepts to a visual plan

Subject Matter

Social Studies
Math
Art
Language arts

Vocabulary Words

plan   **model**
scale   **proportion**

Time

Teacher: One-half hour to prepare chart
Students: One 45- to 60-minute classroom session

Materials

One 12" × 18" sheet of green or dark blue construction paper for each student

Sheets of red, yellow, orange, brown, and light blue construction paper
Rulers
Pencils
Scissors
Glue

Copies for each student of the "Space Bubble" sheet (page 119)
One 1-1/2" white circle for each student

Preparation

Make a chart on a large sheet of paper, similar to example Sheet 1, that illustrates the various bubble sizes, their names, and the color key.

Procedure

Introduction to the students:

> You have all had fun blowing soap bubbles, haven't you? Think about how that clear, crystal-like bubble looked as it floated out through space.

> Think about how you would look floating around inside that bubble. Now bring your bubble down on the ground and think about how you would look walking around on the ground in it.

> Some experts have done research that has supported the idea that we all have imaginary bubbles around us. They vary in size according to the activities that we do in them.

If you have done the activity People Spaces: How Much Room Do You Need?, refer to it and hand-out copies of sheet "Space Bubbles."

> These various bubbles are above us, below us, and all around us. That is, they are three dimensional. They can stand still or they can move around.

> Today we are going to make a **plan** of the way the bubbles are located in our room. A plan can only show the things that are on the floor below the level of our arms when we stretch them out to our sides. (Demonstrate.) A plan is just two dimensional. It only can show length and width. We will cut an imaginary slice through our imaginary bubble. Think about cutting a slice across an apple.

> Now imagine cutting a slice across your bubble. That slice is what will be shown on the plan.

Hand out the sheets of green or dark blue paper.

> This will be the size of your plan. You can't make a drawing the actual size of the room, can you? Instead you will have to draw it in a smaller **scale.** Architects make drawings for buildings to scale. That means that they make a small drawing that has been measured so

that it is the same size, proportionally, as the actual size of the room. When you make a **model** of an airplane or car, what are you doing? Right. You are making the model in a small scale that is in **proportion** to the real thing. (This material will be review if students have done the activity, What Do You See Here? in Tuning into the Environment.)

A good scale for what you are doing right now is 1/2 inch equals 1 foot. (Point it out on the chart.) This sheet of 12-inch by 18-inch paper, at a scale of 1/2 inch equals 1 foot, would represent a room 24 feet by 36 feet. The size of this room is 20 feet by 32 feet (or whatever the size is). Use your ruler to lay out the size of the room at a scale of 1/2 inch to 1 foot. For instance, one half of 20 feet would be 10 feet, so that would be 10 inches at this scale on your paper. One half of 32 feet would be what? Take a measurement at two places on each side. Put your ruler on the two marks and draw a line. This way your line should be straight. Cut out your floor plan.

The first bubble that will be put on the floor plan is the public bubble. Look on the chart. How far does that bubble extend out all around you? Twelve to twenty-five feet in each direction. That will be almost the whole room. What color is this bubble to be? Yes, brown.

Hand out sheets of brown paper.

Let's make this bubble an average size that will fit the room space. Your room is a rectangular shape so make one side longer than the other. One dimension could be 18 feet. That is, between 12 and 25 feet. At a scale of 1/2 inch equals 1 foot, how many inches will 18 feet be? That is right, it will be nine inches. Let's assume that you are standing right in the middle of this sheet.

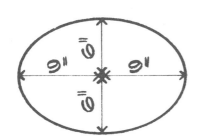

Fold your paper so the edges meet on the long side. Open it up and do the same on the short side. Where the lines cross is where you should put a dot that represents you in the room. If you have folded carefully the dot will be in the center of the room. Lay your ruler on the dot and measure out nine inches from it in one direction on the long way of the sheet. Be sure to make a mark on the paper for each measurement.

Illustrate these instructions on a chart.

Now lay the ruler on the paper in the opposite direction and measure the same way. The paper isn't quite wide

enough, is it? But your room is a little longer than it is wide so your public bubble might take on a similar shape. Bubbles aren't always completely round. An average distance *in* this direction might be only twelve feet. That would be six inches in this scale. Lay your ruler on the dot and measure six inches in the opposite direction. Draw a light line through the four marks you have on your paper in a bubble shape. When you think the bubble looks about right, draw the line in heavier, so you can see it better, and cut out the bubble. Label it *Public Bubble* along one edge.

Place your bubble on the piece of paper that represents the floor plan and paste it down. It takes up almost all the space in the room, doesn't it? What kinds of activities take place in the big bubble? (Teacher instructions, films, tests, etc.)

Within this public bubble lots of other things happen that fit into smaller size bubbles. To decide where they will be placed, you need to notice where other things are located in the room. Look at your floor plan. Put the paper on your desk so that the long dimension is in the long dimension of the room. Where is the door located? When you are sure that you have it in the right place, draw an arrow pointing to it and label it with the word *door*.

Look around again. Where are the windows? Are they opposite the door? Are they on the wall along side the door? Do they take up the whole wall or just a part of it? How many of them are there? When you are sure you have the right location, draw an arrow for each one and label them with the word *window*. Locate anything else that is a permanent part of the room such as a sink, cupboards, or bookcases. Draw arrows and label them. You may want to move the teacher's desk around, so don't draw it in.

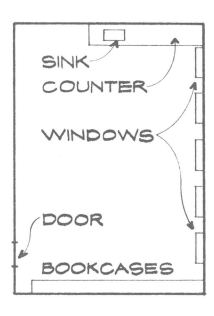

Now you have your plan view of the room pretty well laid out and you are ready for the next bubble. It is the casual bubble. How big is it? Look at the chart. It extends from seven to twelve feet out on all sides. Let's say this one will be nine feet out for us.

Hand out sheets of light blue paper.

How many inches will nine feet be in our scale of one-half inch equals a foot? Right. It will be four and one-half inches. Do the same as you did before. Put a dot on paper and measure four and one-half inches out from it in all directions and mark each measurement. Fold the paper as you did before if it helps you to make the measurements. Draw a bubble-shaped line that goes through all the marks then cut your bubble out. You may want one or two more of this bubble, so you can use this one as a pattern. Write *Casual Bubble* on the edge of each one.

The casual bubble is where you may work independently, sharpen your pencil, get a book off the shelf or mix paints at the sink. In this area you don't feel that you have to talk with anyone else unless you want to. Look your plan over. Where do you think the casual bubble areas might be?

Press for answers such as the bookcases, the storage areas, the sink area, the blackboards, or display areas. When the students have rached a general agreement about the number and location of the bubbles say. . .

Cut out the other bubbles you will need and place them on your plan. Remember to look at the other things on your plan—the doors, windows, and bookcases—and place these bubbles in the right locations in relation to them.

Let's take a look at the chart again. Which color do we need for the next bubble? Orange.

Hand out sheets of orange paper.

What is the name of this bubble? (The social bubble.) What size is it? Yes, from four feet to seven feet out in all directions. You're a pretty sociable bunch so let's make a pretty big bubble for this one. Let's use an average of six feet out all around. How many inches will that be in our scale? Yes, it will be three inches. Mark your dot and measure out three inches in each direction. Make the marks and draw the bubble line. Cut it out. Label the bubble.

Now you have a plan of a social bubble. This is the space in which you have small group discussions, work in special learning groups or ask questions of the teacher. Where would these spaces be in our classroom?

Press for answers such as a work table area, the teacher's desk, a particular desk arrangement, etc.

It is harder to identify these spaces? Do they change quite often? Why? Sometimes creating social bubble areas in the classroom may not be the most desireable thing to do. The use of these spaces needs to be clearly defined so they are not abused. These bubbles may move around the room at times when certain special tasks are to be accomplished.

Are you having trouble making them fit? What is happening here? Are they overlapping? That is all right. Room areas can be multi-purpose; that is, they can have more than one use. Making this bubble plan helps you see which areas those are. As you glue them down, let them overlap but don't cover any bubble completely.

Your plans are looking very nice, but we still have two more bubbles to go. What is the next one? (The friendly bubble.) What color is it? (Yellow.)

Hand out sheets of yellow paper.

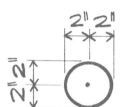

How big is this bubble? That's right, it is from one foot six inches to four feet out in all directions. You like to be friendly so let's make it the biggest size. Make it an average of four feet out. How many inches will that be in our scale? Yes, it will be two inches. Make the dot and measure two inches out in each direction. Make the marks and draw the bubble as you did before. Cut it out and label it.

This is the bubble space for your family and close friends. It is the space for private conversations, sharing lunch, or planning to do something special over the week-end. Think, for a moment, about who would be in your friendly bubble. Some of them, like your family, won't be in this classroom. How many do you think can get in it? Remember the size. You and your friends won't be comfortable if it is too crowded. You are probably more apt to be in your friendly bubble out on the playground at recess when you can get together with your friends. You can't do that most of the time in the classroom, can you? In fact, you may get in trouble if you don't stay out of your friendly bubble during class time! Are there some places for this bubble in the classroom?

Answers might be a "reading corner, a loft, or an area with pillows and carpet." A friendly bubble might be some space where two or three friends can get together to play a game or share a book at certain times as a treat for having their work done. If there isn't such a spot, this would be a good time to discuss creating one and deciding where it might be located.

We have one more bubble. You have done your measuring very well so this one will be made easy for you. Here is your own personal bubble all cut out for you. This bubble is one foot six inches out from your skin on all sides. That is three-quarters of an inch in our scale, so it will look like this.

Hand out a 1-1/2-inch diameter circle to each student.

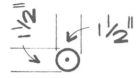

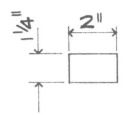

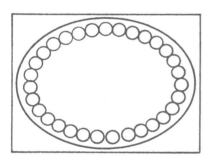

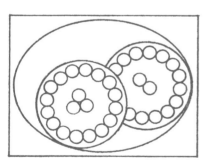

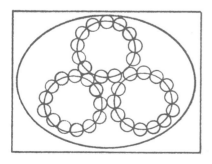

Each one of you carries this bubble around with you all the time. You move it in and out of other larger bubbles as you walk around. It may change shape when you sit down, stretch out on the floor or play ball, but it is always there. Draw a face on it that looks like you.

Since each of you has one of these bubbles, how many will there be in this room? Right—as many bubbles as there are students. The chart says that the others should be red.

Hand out sheets of red paper.

Use your bubble as a pattern for the others. Draw around the pattern, keeping the bubbles close together so you can get them all on the sheet of paper. You will need to make a cutout for the teacher's desk, too. It is about two feet six inches by four feet, so measure two inches one way and one and one-quarter inch the other. Draw a rectangle through the marks and cut it out.

Put your own bubble where your desk is. Put the teacher's desk in the proper location. Be sure to get it in the right place in relation to the doors and windows. Now put all the other bubbles in the right locations for all the other desks. Now you have a floor plan of the room the way it is arranged now. Look at it in relation to all the various bubbles and how they indicate what the space is used for. Is this a good workable plan for the use of the classroom? Does it work well for the teacher?

Let's move the bubbles around a little. Use the public bubble to determine the room arrangement, putting all the desks around the edge of the biggest bubble. How would that work when you were showing a film, or the teacher was giving instructions, or for small group work?

Now try putting the desks in the casual bubbles. Will you have to leave some people outside the bubble or crowded in the middle? How about getting to the sink or the bookcases?

Arrange the desks in the social bubbles. You may have to crowd the desks close together or push them out from the bubble edges a little to get everyone in. Place the teacher's desk in a good location. This plan looks quite nice. How do you think it would work?

Let's try the last bubble. Put all the desks into friendly bubbles. You notice that four personal bubbles fit very nicely. You may need to imagine a few more friendly bubbles in order to fit all the desks in the plan in

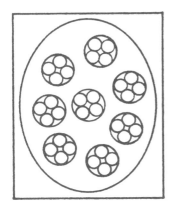

groups of four. What does your plan look like now? Does it remind you of a restaurant with four people at each table? Eating is a friendly activity so this is often the way a restaurant is arranged. It would be good for a party in the classroom too. What are some of the advantages of this kind of an arrangement? What are the problems? How could you solve them?

You have some experience with the bubbles now. Could you make another plan that might work just as well or better than the way the room is arranged now. Move your desk/bubbles around to create a new arrangement. Think about the larger bubbles in relation to your new plan. Think about the location of the permanent things in the room and of the teacher's desk. When you have a plan that you think really works within the space, paste all the bubbles down.

Closure

Display the plans and discuss the spatial arrangements. Point out such things as . . .

Why are so many classrooms arranged with the teacher in front in the middle of the room and the desks spread out in rows facing the teacher's desk? Everyone is in eye contact with the teacher and at the outer edge of each other's friendly bubble. It is a good arrangement for keeping order in the classroom but it isn't very interesting.

Arrangements where four or six people are grouped together are good for group work and are very pleasant. They allow people to be helpful to one another. However, it does require good self-discipline to keep from talking too much.

The public bubble is good for listening but not for interaction. The casual bubble is not as good for listening and would be difficult for class discussion because some people have their backs to others. The desks would probably be moved for discussion or for small group work. The social bubble would have some of the same problems.

Semi-circles and U-shapes work well for large group discussions because everyone has eye contact with most everyone else and it leaves a nice open space in the middle.

Grouping the desks together in some way leaves more space to move around and to do special activities, but some people just can't concentrate when other people are too close to them. Some people have to be against the wall in a corner so that no one will get into their friendly bubble if they are going to get any work done at all.

Now that you know the sizes of the various bubbles, you will be able to understand why some kinds of activities work in one space and not in another. You will know how much room you need for certain activities. You will know why some spaces are arranged the way they are so that specific activities will happen in them. You can even cause activities to happen by creating the right space for them. Knowing the distances can help in the development of a good plan.

Analyze the plans and select two or three that seem to work well. Arrange the room according to one of the plans. Leave it that way for a week and record what happens in relation to the bubble distances. Use each of the other arrangements for a week and analyze them. Compare them all at the end of the experimental period.

SPACE BUBBLE CHART

DIMENSIONS SHOWN HERE INDICATE AVERAGE
SIZES BETWEEN THE DESCRIBED LIMITS

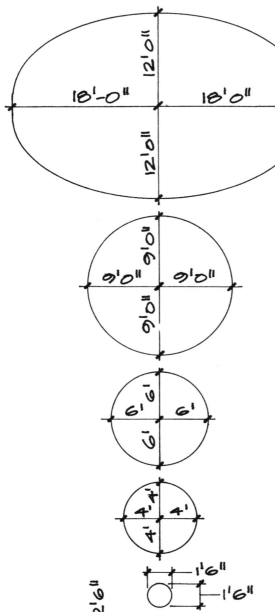

CHART SCALE 1/12" = 1'-0"

A SHEET OF GREEN OR DARK
BLUE PAPER SHOULD REPRE-
SENT THE WHOLE ROOM.

PUBLIC BUBBLE
12 FEET TO 25 FEET
BROWN SAMPLE TO REPRESENT
AVERAGE SIZE OF 12' x 18'
SCALE SIZE 9" x 6"

CASUAL BUBBLE
7 FEET TO 12 FEET
LIGHT BLUE SAMPLE REPRE-
SENTING AVERAGE SIZE OF
9' x 9'
SCALE SIZE 4½" x 4½"

SOCIAL BUBBLE
4 FEET TO 7 FEET
ORANGE SAMPLE REPRESENT-
ING AVERAGE SIZE OF 6' x 6'
SCALE SIZE 3" x 3"

FRIENDLY BUBBLE
1 FOOT 6 INCHES TO 4 FEET
YELLOW SAMPLE REPRESENT-
ING THE FULL 4 FEET
SCALE SIZE 2" x 2"

PERSONAL BUBBLE
FROM SKIN TO 1 FOOT 6 INCHES
RED SAMPLE REPRESENTING
THE FULL SIZE
SCALE SIZE 3/4" x 3/4"

THE TEACHER'S DESK CAN BE
RED BECAUSE THE SHAPE
DIFFERS.
SCALE SIZE 1¼" x 2"

NOTE: THE BUBBLES FOR
THE ACTUAL CHART SHOULD
BE DRAWN AT A SCALE OF
½" = 1'0" AS ILLUSTRATED
IN THE LESSON PLAN.

SCHOOL SPACES

Theme

The school environment is the most easily accessible one for the student to study. Because it is encountered daily, often there is little awareness of details. Measuring and drawing a floor plan of the school provides many opportunities for studying this environment.

Learning Objectives

To utilize techniques for measurement and recording
To understand drawing in scale and converting measurements
To gain ability in group cooperation

Subject Matter

Social Studies
Math
Art

Time

One 45- to 60-minute classroom session for introduction
One session for measurements

Vocabulary Words

plan	**scale**
record	**sketch**
spaces	**process**
architect	**brainstorming**
design criteria	

Materials

Copies of "How to Measure a Room" and "Symbols to Use in Drawing a Floor Plan I-III for each group (see pgs 48–51)
Graph paper in 1/4" squares
Large sheet of butcher paper (at a scale of 1/4" = 1'0", a distance of 100 feet will require 25 inches of paper) Locate the office on the sheet so the students will have a point of reference.
Pencils
Rulers

Possibly some parental help

A set of the architectural plans of the school (if possible). Do not show them to the students until after they have finished their plan.

Procedure

Inform the rest of the school staff that your students will be measuring the school.

Introduction to the students.

Drawing a **plan** of the school is a good way to learn about the school environment. When we see something every day we take it for granted and often don't even notice some things about it. Sometimes something is changed and, while we may notice that something is different, we can't remember what was there before. For instance, what is in the display case right now (or on the wall or in the office)? What was there before?

Becoming really aware of the environment around us takes practice and a knowledge of some techniques for helping us see more. Drawing pictures is one good way to do that. Another is drawing a plan. By the time you finish this plan you will know a lot more about the school than you do now. Maybe you will find some places you didn't know existed or maybe you will find some that shouldn't exit! Do you think there are any secret hideouts in this school?

Don't get worried, you won't each draw the whole school. You will work in groups and each group will measure a certain portion of the school. They will **record** their measurements and then lay out the **spaces** they have measured on paper. Then each group will put their drawings on this large sheet of paper in the proper locations. We will hope that it will all fit together.

That may be a problem. If different groups are going to do different areas, maybe we need to decide on a few rules before we start. What might they be?

Press for answers such as . . .

how to divide up the areas
how to take the measurements
how to record the measurements
how the drawings are going to be made
how to decide what size all the drawings should be

These are all very important considerations if we are going to have a good result. An **architect** would call these things the **design criteria.** Let's establish some design criteria for this project. Here is the big piece of paper that you will put all your drawings on. The office is located on the plan so you will have an idea where to start.

Measure and draw the plan of the office on the graph paper and paste it in the approximate location on the sheet that will allow the plan to grow around it. If there isn't time for doing this just write the word *office* in the location.

Deciding on the size you will use to make the drawings is probably the most important thing to be done. When architects draw plans for buildings they very often use a **scale** of 1/4 inch equals 1 foot. They would write it like this (indicate it on hand-out sheet): Scale 1/4″ = 1′0″. That scale is about right for showing rooms, built-ins, cabinets, closets, plumbing fixtures, and all sorts of things like that. If this is your first experience with drawing a plan in scale, you can use graph paper that has 1/4-inch squares. At the scale you are going to use, what will each square equal? (One foot.)

See Ruler at Various Scales (page 182) for a simplified method of measurement.

You will draw all the spaces in the school—the rooms, halls, closets, storage areas, heating room, etc. After you have all the areas that have been assigned to your group drawn on the graph paper, each group will tape them on the big sheet in the right locations.

A floor plan shows only what is on the floor. Stand up and stretch your arms out to your sides. Imagine you are a bird flying over the room at just the height of your arms and you are looking straight down on the floor. Architectural floor plans are always drawn looking at the floor this way. It was something agreed on a long time ago so that anyone who reads them will understand them. A plan shows everything that is on the floor below the level of your arms. It is as if a slice has been cut through the room the same way you might cut across an apple. A plan of the apple would only show what you can see in the bottom half.

If students have done the activity What Do You See Here? (page 42) the following discussion may be omitted.

Look around the room. Remember that you are looking straight down on it. You will only see the top of the counters, not the doors below. The sink will just be a rectangle. The windows will just be lines as though you see only the edge of the glass. The doors will be openings in the walls. Will the walls be just one line? Why not? What would you see if you sliced through a wall? There might be wood or concrete block between the wall finishes on either side, so you will draw two lines. Walls are about six inches thick, so how far apart will your lines be? (One half of a square.) What will happen when two rooms are next to each other? Do you have two walls? (No, only one wall that both rooms share.) Refer to your sheets, "Symbols to Use in Drawing a Floor Plan," to find out how to draw such things as walls and doors on your plan.

Now, let's talk about how we will take the measurements.

If the students have done the Pacing activity (page 180) and have established their individual pace, this is a good time to use it. It will make the measuring go much faster than when using the yardstick or tape measure, and the results will probably be almost as accurate. The goal is to increase awareness, so don't be too demanding about the accuracy of the measurements. Locating the rooms, halls, etc., in their proper relationships to one another is important, however.

When you start measuring a room, make a rough **sketch** of it on a piece of scratch paper. Mark the location of the door so you will know which measurement goes where. Refer to your sheet, "How to Measure a Room."

Here is how to record your measurements. Write each one down as soon as you take it. Label the things in the room as you measure them. Be sure to write the name or number of the room. If you don't write everything down as you do it you will forget or get mixed up. This is where the group helps. Have one person writing the measurements down. Other people can measure various parts. You should always have to people measure each thing so you can compare and check the results. If they aren't almost the same then you should check it out a third time. If this is all going to fit together well, you will have to try to be very careful about the measurements.

Optional

Since you have already established your individual pace, this would be a good time to make use of it. It will make the larger measurements go more quickly. Practice your pace again so you get the rhythm going evenly. Two people pace off the area and compare their numbers. Remember your pace is in inches so you will need to convert the measurements into feet and inches before putting it on your plan. How do you do that? Yes, you multiply the number of paces times the length of your pace. The answer will be in inches so you will divide by 12 to put it in feet. Do your figuring on the scratch paper so it can be checked. For the smaller measurements the yardstick will work better, but still mark them down in feet and inches. Another thing about drawing a good plan is to be consistent— to do everything the same way throughout the plan.

You may want to use several sheets of paper for the different areas so your sketches will be big enough to get all the figures on them so they can be easily read.

Divide the students in working groups, assign the areas each group is to measure, and send them out. This would be a good opportunity to use some parent help in supervising the groups both in the measuring and the drawing.

Have the 1/4-inch graph paper available when the students return. Encourage the use of rulers in preference to counting squares. If a room is 32 feet long, it is quicker to measure 8 inches with a ruler than it is to count 32 squares. It also increases the understanding of the use of ruler in making scale drawings or maps.

When quite a few of the groups have their plan drawings complete, start having them place them on the large plan sheet. Use masking tape temporarily so that changes can be made as they see mistakes or realize that something is missing. If some areas are really out of scale have them measure again and/or redraw.

Have all the students look over the completed plan to identify the problems, make changes and additions, and get the plan as correct as possible. Then glue everything in place.

Closure

When the plan is complete, initiate a discussion.

What was the hardest part of getting this plan together? Will it be easier for you to draw a plan of something else now? What have you learned about drawing plans? What have you learned about the school that you didn't know before? What have you learned about working together on a project?

Having to investigate an environment using some kind of **process** for making observations helps people to see more of what is there to be seen. In this case drawing the plan was the process both for making the observations and for recording them so others could understand them. Working together in groups gets more work done and the group benefits from the skills of each of its members. On this project some of you drew well, some were good at measuring, and some were good at the math needed for converting inches to feet.

Groups working together can get much more done in causing environmental change or keeping something from changing. In developing environmental awareness, you all have something to contribute and something to learn from others. When you know some techniques such as measuring and drawing plans, you have some tools that can be used very effectively.

This activity makes an excellent base from which to proceed with **brainstorming** about creating some visual change in the school and developing a project that the students can implement.

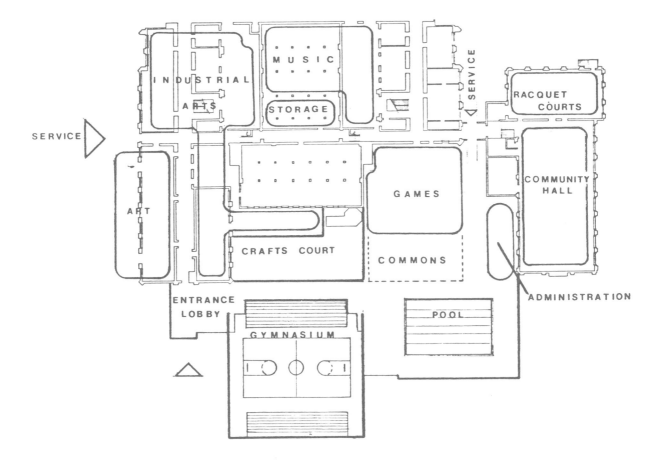

4 STRUCTURE AND SPACE

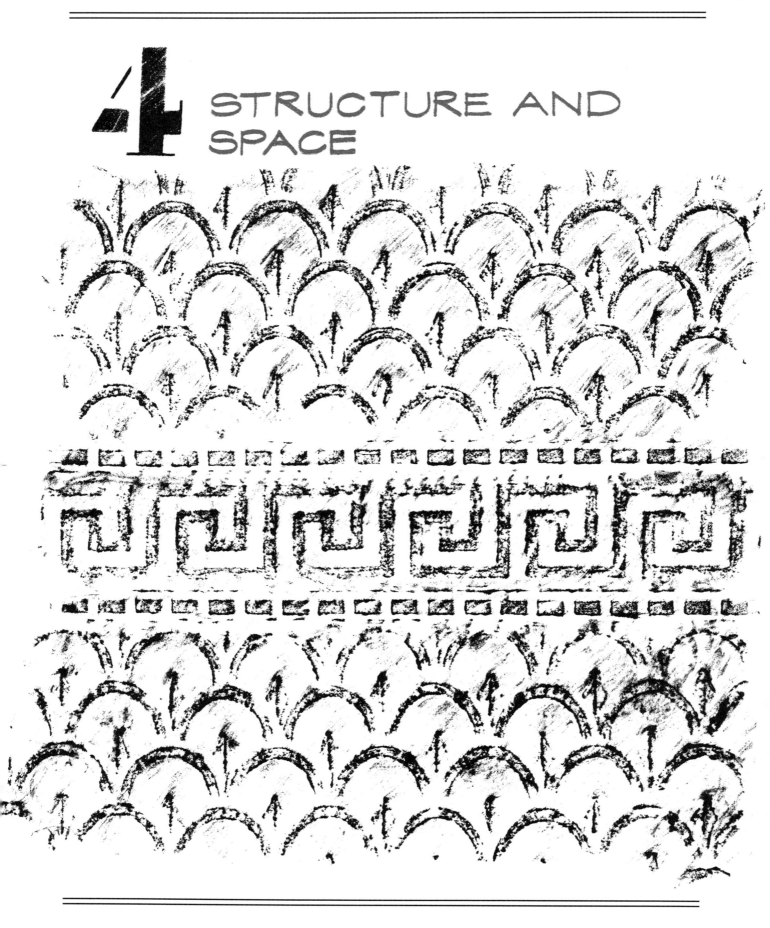

INTRODUCTION

Theme

Within the school curriculum there are many ways of developing environmental awareness that, at the same time, add interest and increased understanding of the subject matter. This series of activities are primarily related to mathematics. Used in the manner suggested, they provide a visual system for discovering new forms and insights in the surrounding world.

The Activities

1. How It Feels to Be a Structure
2. Carrying the Load
3. Shapes for Enclosing a Space
4. Creating New Shapes for Enclosing Space
5. Building a "Time-out" Space
6. Thoughts About a Space

These activities provide a sense of structure and the strength of construction members, an application of principles and awareness of spatial concepts, and an experience with a continuing process leading to a visual result.

Curriculum Areas

Math and Science through measurement, working with geometric shapes and structures and spatial concepts

Social Studies through understanding of a process for the accomplishment of a goal and group decision making and cooperation

Language Arts through many new vocabulary words and creative writing

Art and Industrial Arts through drawing, learning new techniques and use of tools, and an appreciation of the aesthetic qualities in mathematical forms

Where

These activities are all to be done in the classroom.

Why

Utilizing some quite sophisticated mathematical concepts to build models, to build a full-size space structure, and as a system for making notations about the environment provide an exciting visual application. This can be very stimulating to the students interested in mathematics and understanding of it. The culmination in the building of a structure reinforces:

The value of a step-by-step procedure

The belief that something that is conceptualized can become a reality; this is something that most students seem quite skeptical about

The concept of learning through transference from one thing (a model) to another (a full-size structure)

Extensions

The process can be repeated for a different project or model.

The cardboard structure could become the pattern for a more permanent structure in wood.

Bibliography

Polyhedron Models by Magnus J. Wenninger. Cambridge University Press, New York, 1976.

Photographs, patterns, and instructions are give for 119 polyhedra. Students would be fascinated looking through it.

Cathedral—The Story of Its Construction by David Macaulay. Houghton Mifflin Company, Boston, 1973.

A story, written for young people and illustrated with beautiful drawings, shows the application of many of the concepts covered in the Structure and Space activities.

HOW IT FEELS TO BE A STRUCTURE

Theme

The concepts concerning the structural properties of various geometric shapes and how this knowledge can be a part of every day life are hard for a student to grasp. These concepts can become exciting when students are involved in activities that use their bodies to actually "feel" how it is to be a beam, a column, or a truss.

Learning Objectives

To gain understanding of mathematical principles through sensory perception
To relate mathematics to real life situations

Subject Matter

Math
Science
Language Arts

Vocabulary Words

architect	tension
contractor	arch
beam	post
support	column
load	compression
span	truss
laminated beam	balance
deflection	geometrically stable
structural failure	overload
safety factor	structure
warp	dome
structural members	triangle
reinforcement	

Time

Teacher: Forty-five minutes to assemble materials
Students: Forty-five to sixty minutes in the classroom

Materials

Using a projector cart as a base works well because the

materials can be stored on the lower shelf and put on top for good viewing, as they are needed.

Assemble:

Seventeen lightweight cardboard strips 1-1/2″ wide and 15″ long. Set six of the strips aside.

Fold the others and tape them to form a circle, a square, a rectangle, three arches, and five equilateral triangles.

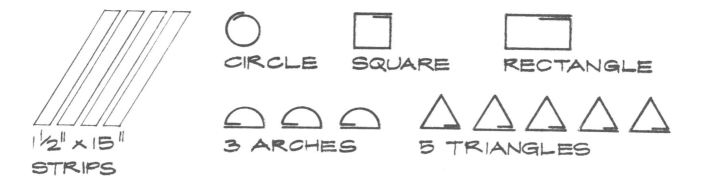

1½″ × 15″ STRIPS   CIRCLE   SQUARE   RECTANGLE

3 ARCHES   5 TRIANGLES

A square box and a rectangular box (small)
Six or eight furniture casters or other small weights

Preparation

Prior to the classroom session:
Practice the activity to experience the steps and to check on your materials to be sure they are going to work well.

Make any adjustments necessary.

Procedure

In the classroom session:
Explain to the students:

> Today we are going to talk about how buildings are built. When an **architect** designs a building and a **contractor** builds it, what subject do you think it is important that they know?

Press the questions until you get the answer "mathematics."

> That's right, knowing about mathematics can make a big difference when you are building something. Have you ever built a fort or a playhouse? What happened to it?

Usually someone will say, "It fell down."

Do you have any ideas on how mathematics might have helped you? There are lots of things that math can do to help us build things so they won't fall down. Let's look at some of them.

As you say each of the underlined words, which deal with the mathematical properties of a structure, write them on a chart.

Put the two boxes on top of the cart 10 inches to 12 inches apart. Lay one of the straight strips across them, tape the ends down and place a weight in the center.

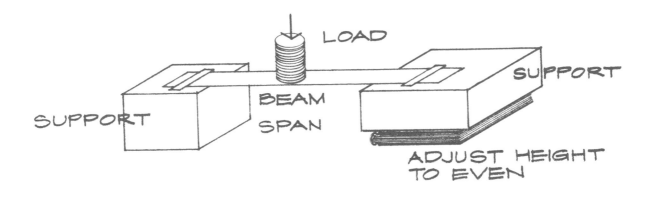

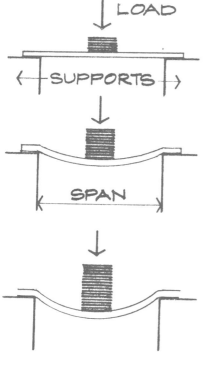

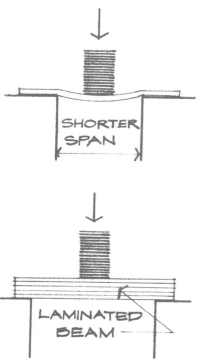

When you build something, one of the first things that you will have to deal with is putting **beams** between **supports.**

Indicate the elements in the example as you say the words.

In this case the boxes are the supports ang taping the ends down is similar to nailing a beam in place. The distance between the supports is called the **span.** The weight in the middle is called the **load.** We are going to experiment with adding more load to the beam and see what happens.

If we were going to use math to figure out how to keep this beam from breaking, we would need some information. We would need to know

How heavy the load is
How big the beam should be for that load
How far apart the supports can be in relation to the span of the beam

As we don't have all that information, we will just have to play around here and see what happens when we increase the load on the beam.

Add the weights, one at a time, until the beam begins to sag.

Is the beam changing? What is happening? Yes, the beam is beginning to sag, to curve downward, isn't it?

Add all the weights you have.

If this was a beam in your house and it curved down too much, you might hit your head on it or the ceiling might fall on you. What could you do to keep that from happening? (Make it bigger or put the supports closer together.)

Move the supports close together, until the beam remains fairly straight under the load.

That helps, but if we did that in our living room the supports might be too close together to leave room for a couch or table. Maybe we had better try making the beam bigger. We don't have any heavier cardboard, so what could we do? (Add more layers.)

Lay the other five strips on the beam and tape them together, then put the weights on again.

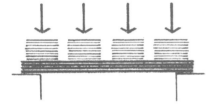

That makes it stronger, doesn't it? When we layer strips of material and fasten them together, we have a **laminated beam.** Wood beams are often laminated.

Turn the strips so they rest on edge and put the weights on.

This beam is even stronger when the load is put on the edge of the strips. The wood in laminated beams is usually on edge.

There is another thing that we can do to keep the beam from sagging too much. We can spread the load out. Instead of putting the weights all in one place we can put them all along the beam.

Place the weights all along the beam to show how dispersing the load reduces the downward curve.

This downward curve, or sag, is another thing that can be figured out with math. It is called the **deflection** and you can find out just how much a beam of a certain size and material will deflect under a certain load.

Would you like to find out how it feels to be a beam that deflects?

Place two chairs just far enough apart that a student can stretch between them with the head on one chair and the feet on the other.

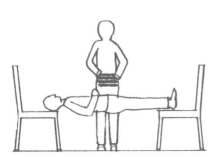

Who would like to be a beam? You will need to span yourself between the chairs.

Have the student get in position then have the other students load books on the "beam's" stomach. Comment on the deflection as it begins to occur. When it looks as though no more weight can be held, or the students actually falls down, you can point out . . .

> Our beam has reached the limit of it's ability to carry a load. It has reached the point of **structural failure.**

Let other students have the experience or suggest that they try it at recess.

> What could we have done that might have made the beam hold up a little longer? (Spread the load.)

> It is possible to figure out just what the point of structural failure will be but, even so, architects, engineers, and contractors like to be very sure that their buildings won't fall down. They always make them a little stronger than the figures tell them is necessary. This is called building in a **safety factor.** That would be like finding out how many books your beam could hold without any deflection and then removing a few of them to provide a safety factor.

> Well, now you know something about how it feels to be a beam. Where are there beams in this room? (Over the door and window or openings and in the ceiling.)

> Now let's look at some other shapes that are used in buildings and find out some things that it might be helpful to know about them.

Set up the strips made into the square and the rectangle. Press your finger on the top of each.

> When you **overload** these shapes they begin to move sideways—they **warp.** They too reach a point of structural failure when they are loaded too heavily. They could warp so much that they would completely flatten out. That wouldn't be so good if you were inside, would it? Can you think of something we could do to keep that from happening?

Hold the rectangle or the square against the side of one of the boxes and put a load on it.

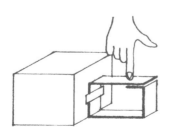

> What is happening now? Yes, the box is giving the shape support. When you put a wall at a right angle to another wall, they are both strengthened—they give each other support. Another way to describe this is to say they **reinforce** each other.

> Why don't you see how it feels to be a support, or **reinforcement.** Stand with your body against the wall. Press your shoulder, elbow, hip, and foot against the wall. You are a wall helping to support another wall.

Face the wall and rest your hands against it. Now push hard against the wall. That feels different, doesn't it? You have tightened up. That is called **tension.** When **structural members** are in tension with one another, they become very strong.

Bring out the boxes again.

When you put squares and rectangles together to form a box, they become very strong and can hold a lot of weight.

Press down on the tops and then the sides.

They don't warp to one side or the other. What is the shape of this room? Yes, most rooms are three-dimensional squares or rectangles (box-shaped) and now you can see why. The sides of the box reinforce each other. Look around this room and think of it as a box with all the sides—the walls, ceiling, and floor—working together to reinforce each other.

Bring out the circle.

Do we use circles very much in building?

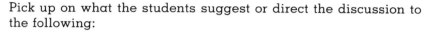

Pick up on what the students suggest or direct the discussion to the following:

> Not too often because a circle doesn't sit on the ground or the floor too well, so it isn't very **stable.** It might roll away like a hoop.

Roll the circle along the table. Press your finger down on the top of the circle.

> When I put some weight—a load—on the circle it begins to change shape, doesn't it? It doesn't warp in the same way the square or the rectangle did. What is it becoming? (It is flattening out into an ellipse.) If the load is really heavy, what could it do? (Flatten clear out and become a strip.)

> There is a way that we use a circle quite often in building. Can you think of how that is? (Windows.) What about using half of it? (Arches.)

Bring out the strips that have been made into an arch.

What do we call something that looks like this? It is an **arch** and it is a very pretty shape in a building. It also works much better than a circle when you load it.

Press down on the center or an arch.

However, when you press too hard it begins to flatten out. What do we call it when it does that? Right. Deflection. Let's see what we could do about that. Remember when we put squares or rectangles together and the **structure** became much stronger? What could we do here? Yes, we could put several of these arches together.

Tape the arches together. Press down on the top.

The arches are stronger now, aren't they? Why? (Because they are reinforcing each other.) What do we call a structure that looks like this? Right, it is called a **dome.** A dome is stronger than a single arch.

Is there somebody here who can do a good back bend?

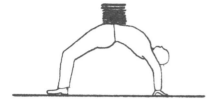

Okay, we are going to have you tell use how it feels to be an arch.

Have the student hold the back bend as long as possible while the others pile on the books until deflection or structural failure occurs. For those who cannot do a back bend, a less spectacular demonstration can be done facing the floor with hands and feet touching the floor and the back arched.

What did you do when the books were piled on? Did you tense your muscles? Remember when you pushed against the wall with your hands so you would know how it feels to support a wall? You tensed your muscles then, too. What was the word we used for that? Right. Tension. When we make an arch with a strip we are creating tension.

Bend a yardstick into an arch. Let go of one end.

See how the yardstick springs back when I let go of one end? That is because I have released the tension. This yardstick will support more weight when it is made into an arch than it does when it is straight. That is because the tension has added strength to the material.

What else could we do with a circle that would hold a lot of weight? How about a tube? What kind of a building support have you seen that looks like a tube? Yes, a **post.**

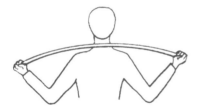

Roll a piece of paper into a tube and tape the edges together.

This may look like a tube, but if it is part of a structure it would be called a post or a **column.**

Press your hand down on the tube. Add weights to the tube.

It doesn't deflect, does it? But if I press quite hard it begins to crunch.

Press on the tube until it starts to collapse.

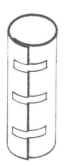

This is a different kind of pressure caused by a load. It is called **compression.** If I put enough compression in this tube or post, I could flatten it out. It is also possible to figure out just how much compression weight a structure can support.

This one is going to be easier for you than the back bend. All you have to do is stand up. I think you can all do that!

Have part of the students stand very straight while the others pile books on their heads.

This is what it feels like to be a post or a column with

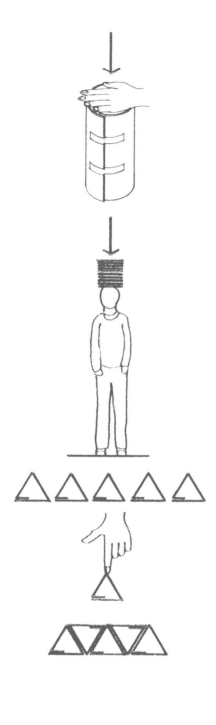

a compression load. Concentrate on how the load feels. What else are you discovering about a load? Yes, if the load isn't put on carefully, it may fall off. If it is off **balance** it changes the ability of the support to carry the load.

Let them take turns experiencing the feeling.

Where have you seen posts or arches in buildings? We have talked about beams, squares, rectangles, circles, arches, posts, and columns. What shape is missing here? Right, it is the **triangle.** It is a very important one because there is something about it that is different from all the others.

Bring out the five triangles. Press your finger down on the point of one of them.

When I load the triangle at the point it doesn't deflect or warp the way the other shapes did. Because of this we say that the triangle is **geometrically stable.** Why would that be important to know if you are building something? That's right, triangles can carry a lot of weight without warping or collapsing. Remember when you were finding out how it felt to be a wall. You couldn't press as hard against the wall when you stood next to it as you could when you stood a little ways away and pushed your hands against the wall. You could feel a lot of tension and force. What shape was your body and the wall forming? (A triangle.)

We have found out that when you put squares, rectangles, circles, or arches together they reinforce each other. That is even more true with triangles.

Place the five triangles together as illustrated.

When we put triangles together like this they become very strong. Have you ever seen anything that looks like this? (A bridge, the roof of the gym or your garage.)

When you put triangles together like this they form what is called a **truss.** Let's find out what it feels like to be a truss.

Sit on the floor with your knees bent up and your hands behind you on the floor. Your body is forming three triangular shapes.

Use one of the students to indicate the triangular shapes.

Now press down hard with your feet and hands. Your muscles have tensed up, haven't they? They are working against each other. Triangles can form a lot of tension. They also provide a way for spreading out the

load, which means that a certain length, or span, can carry a larger load. If we put a beam across your head and knees that would spread out the load. A truss is made up of triangles and beams and sometimes arches. Sometimes the triangular truss is used inside the arch to reinforce it or increase the span.

Show the edge flap of the box or another piece of corrugated cardboard.

Here is another reason why the box is strong. The outside paper is quite thin but it is reinforced by a paper truss inside.

Closure

Now you know that in a sense buildings have "feelings." They tense up their structural muscles to support loads. Their various shapes reinforce each other. When you are walking around the next few days look for "feelings" in this building and in others that you may see in the community. Find three pictures of buildings and outline the areas that illustrate "feelings."

CARRYING THE LOAD

Theme

Assembling construction paper structures and then loading them to the point of failure is an exciting way to experiment with the mathematical properties of geometric shapes. A realistic application of mathematical principles is also demonstrated.

Learning Objectives

To discover some principles that increase the strength of materials and geometric shapes

To experience a graphic demonstration of the strengths and limitations of materials under applied loads.

Subject Matter

Math
Science
Language Arts

Time

Teacher: Fifteen minutes to assemble materials
Students: Forty-five to sixty minutes in the classroom

Vocabulary Words

post	**reinforce**
beam construction	**laminated beam**
span	**concentrated load**
deflection	**arch**
load	**masonry**
cantilever	**keystone**
balance	

Materials

Many pieces of colored construction paper. (This can be a good way to use scraps.) Lightweight cardboard would also be useful.
Masking tape
Scissors
Furniture casters or other small weights

Preparation

This activity is written in a format that allows it to be done as a separate activity, but it would provide a more comprehensive

LOAD

POST AND BEAM CONSTRUCTION

DEFLECTION

CANTILEVER

experience if it was done as a followup to Structure and Space: How It Feels to Be a Structure. References to the activity as this one proceeds will reinforce the learning in each of them.

Gather a box full of assorted sizes of colored construction paper and some full-sized sheets and some cardboard.

Pull off strips of masking tape for each student. See that everyone has a pair of scissors.

Prior to the classroom session:

Have materials for the presentation assembled on a table.

Practice the activity so you will know how the materials are going to work and can make any adjustments necessary.

Procedure

In the classroom session
Explain to the students:

> It is possible to make things out of construction paper that can hold up quite a bit of weight. I am going to do a few little experiments here, just to help you get started, and then I want to see what ideas you can come up with. You will be really surprised, at the end, with the amount of weight you can hold up with paper if you know a few tricks.

> Let's start out by making a **post.** All you need for that is a square or a rectangle. Because I will probably want to make several posts and they should be the same size so they will all help carry a load, I am going to cut six or eight squares six inches by six inches. Now, I will role one of them so I can tape the edges together. When I stand it on end, it looks like a post. I can fold it so it has four sides and now I would have a square post, or I can roll it for a round post.

Stand the two posts up and put a weight on two of them.

> A piece of paper made into a post can hold quite a bit of weight. You have seen lots of round and square posts around you. Can you tell where you have seen them? (There is probably one in the room.)

> We don't usually see a post with a weight on top like this, however. One of the most common ways to build something is called **post and beam construction.** You know that this is the post so what will the beam be? (Something that goes across the top.)

Lay a strip of paper 1 1/2 inch wide and about 18 inches long over the post.

> We seem to have a problem with this beam. What else do we need to hold this up? (More posts.)

LAMINATED BEAM

LAMINATED STRIPS ON EDGE

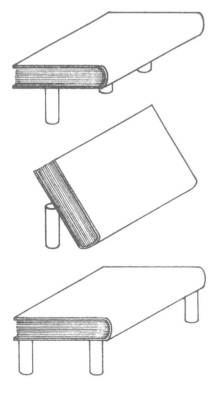

Roll up two or three more posts. Place one at end of the beam, another about a third of the way along the length, and another at the opposite end.

It looks at though our beam is sagging a little on the longer **span.** We call that **deflection.** That won't be very good for carrying much of a weight, or **load.** What could we do about this? (Another post could be added or the beam could be made stronger.)

Both of these ideas would work but let me show you another possibility.

Place the post at about two-thirds of the length of the beam. Gradually snip small pieces from the sagging end of the beam with the scissors until the beam is able to support itself and remain straight out.

Sometimes a beam can extend beyond the post. If it doesn't go too far out, it will still carry quite a load. This kind of extended beam is called a **cantilever.** It is a pretty tricky thing but it can make some spectacular buildings.

Now we see how the posts can be spaced to carry more load, but this paper beam isn't going to hold very much, is it? If we added a whole lot more strips of

paper to the beam it would help some. How about this book? It could probably take quite a load. What is the book made up of? A lot of pages. So that is the same idea as adding more strips.

When you add enough of them, the beam becomes pretty hard to bend, or **deflect,** doesn't it? That is the way a lot of wood beams are made. They are made of strips of wood, glued together. This is called making a **laminated beam.** The strips **reinforce** each other and make it strong. When the wood strips are turned on edge they will carry a greater load than when they are laid flat.

All right, we have a strong beam, but what is apt to happen when I rest it on the three posts?

Place the book on the three posts so that it is a little off center.

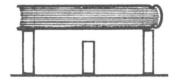

We seem to have another problem. What is it? Right, the book won't **balance.** What do you suggest? (Add more posts and space them in a different way.)

Place four posts under the corners of the book.

Now we can add quite a bit more weight because the four posts are placed so that the load is in balance. There is another reason that it will carry more. Can you figure out what it is? (Because the load is spread out over each of the posts.) When we have a load just on one post, it is called a **concentrated load** and it will need a pretty big post and it would be hard to balance. If it is spread out the load can be heavier and the posts smaller.

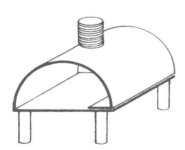

What could you do if you wanted to carry a very large load? (Make bigger posts and have more of them.) Now, here is a tricky one! Can you think of something else that would be important about the posts carrying the load? (They must all be the same height so the load will rest on them equally.)

Architects and engineers know how to mathematically compute just how big the beams need to be and how far apart to put the posts, depending on the load.

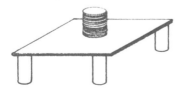

When you put a lot of posts and beams together and fill in the spaces in between them, you get something that looks like a box. That is the way most of our rooms look, isn't it? It is the common way to build because, when you put the walls, floors, and ceilings together you form the box, they all reinforce each other and it makes the building strong.

Sometimes it is sort of refreshing to have rooms that are of different shapes. We often have different shapes for roofs. Let's play around with the **arch** a little. It is a very pleasing shape to look at.

Take a piece of paper about 4 inches by 12 inches. Fold one side 1 inch from the edge. Fold the other side at one third the length of the paper. Tape the edges together and you have an arch—a part of a circle. Place a post under each corner of the arch section. Cut a piece of paper the same size as the base of the arch section and place a post under each corner.

Let's see how the beam and the arch compare when we load them.

Put a weight in the center of them.

Do you see any deflections?

Keep adding weights and making observations.

What does this tell us about arches? (They can be stronger than straight beams.)

We have been putting the load right in the center. Do you remember what we called that? Yes, a concentrated load. How could we make this arch carry a greater load? (Spread the load out so it doesn't all come in one place.) However, an arch doesn't allow you to spread the weight as much as a beam does.

The arch is used a good deal in buildings, not only because it looks nice, but also because it can give more height to an opening or ceiling than a beam can.

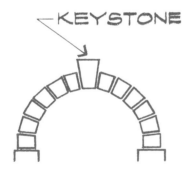

There is another interesting thing about arches. Quite often they are made of **masonry.** That means they are made out of brick or stone. There is a trick for making masonry arches. The bricks or stones are laid up to form the arch with each one slightly angled. When they get to the top they drop in a wedge-shaped piece called a **keystone.** When the keystone is firmly in place, it makes all the stones or bricks work together. Like the laminated strips, they reinforce each other.

Show a picture of a building with an arch and keystone.

There is another trick that will be very helpful to you in your construction.

Fold a piece of paper about 4 inches by 10 inches into several sections, accordion style. Tape the pleated section to two pieces of paper taped to the top and bottom. Begin to apply the weights.

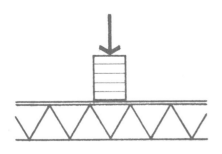

Do you see any deflection here? The paper becomes very strong when you fold it like an accordion. When you look at the end of the paper, it looks like a series of triangles. That's the trick that makes it so strong. Triangles are much stronger than other shapes and when you fasten them together they reinforce each other and can carry a very large load.

So you have seen a number of ways to carry loads. What very important thing did you learn about all of them? (When they are joined, together, they become much stronger, some shapes are stronger than others, etc.)

Let's see how creative you can be about making a structure to carry a load. Use several pieces of paper, your scissors and some masking tape, maybe some cardboard, and see what you can come up with. When you have something put together, we will test it by gradually putting some loads on it.

One rule for this project is that you must combine at least two of the shapes we have talked about in your structure.

While the students are working, walk around making comments to the class when you see something interesting happening. Very soon someone will come up with the idea of putting an accordion-folded piece inside an arched one or clustering the columns together or taping strips of cardboard together to make a beam.

After 20 or 30 minutes, when most everyone has made some shape and loaded it, suggest that they try loading books on their structure, one at a time. Once this suggestion has been made, the competition will quickly begin. As one structure fails under the weight the students see ways they can reinforce it or combine their structures so they can pile on more books. They work up to a pretty tall pile of books. At this point someone usually will think of having a person stand on the structure. Suggest that they put a book over it to spread the load. The ultimate load will probably be the teacher. Stop before it gets out of hand but let them have fun with the experience.

Closure

Well, that turned out to be pretty exciting didn't it? Let's make a list of things that you learned about structures and shapes in this project. (Write the responses on the board and press for as many ideas as possible.)

You have come up with some good comments. How could you learn some more about structures? Yes, you might look at the place where you live. See what you can see down in the basement, up in the attic, or in the garage. You might look around the school, too. One of the best places would be a building under construction. Another idea might be finding pictures in magazines. See if you can find three examples of structures carrying loads between now and tomorrow.

GEOMETRIC SHAPES FOR ENCLOSING SPACE

Theme

Folding geometric shapes into a three-dimensional form which encloses a space is intriguing to students. Coloring the shapes develops a sensitivity to the inate beauty in mathematically conceived forms.

Learning Objectives

To gain skills in three dimensional visualization
To become familiar with several regular polyhedra
To improve motor skills and the ability to follow instructions

Subject Matter

Math
Science
Art
Language Arts

Time

Teacher: One hour to assemble materials and make examples of each model

Students: One or two 45- to 60- minute classroom sessions and perhaps some free time, depending on how many shapes are made. Younger students would probably only do the first three.

Vocabulary Words

geometric shape	**tetrahedron**
closed shapes	**geometrically stable**
space	**hexahedron**
equilateral triangle	**octahedron**
regular polyhedra	**icosahedron**
irregular polyhedra	**cuboctahedron**
pyramid	**reinforce**

Materials

Enough copies of the sheets "Geometric Shapes for Enclosing Space" for each student to make at least one model of each shape and extras for those who work quickly. Sheet 6 will require two copies for each shape.

Scissors
Quick-drying white glue, toothpicks, and a piece of rigid wire
Felt pens or crayons
Strips of cardboard
A small cardboard box

Preparation

Cut out, fold, and glue together an example of each "Geometric Shapes for Enclosing Space"

Fold strips of cardboard into a square, a rectangle, a circle and a triangle, or use examples from How It Feels to Be a Structure.

> What do we mean when we say something is a **geometric shape?**

Show the square, rectangle, circle, and triangle.

> These are geometric shapes. They are also called **closed shapes** because the line that goes around the edge of the shape joins itself. Each of these shapes is also flat. What would we need to do if we wanted to use these shapes to make a fort or a playhouse or a reading space? (Make the strips wider like walls, put a front and back on it.)

Show a box or the model of the cube.

> When you add to the shape so that they enclose some air or **space,** then you have changed the shapes from flat pieces of paper with *two dimensions*—height and width—to shapes that have space inside them. They have *three dimensions*—height, width, and depth. You see this box? It is made up of squares (and / or rectangles) joined together so that they enclose a space. It has height, width, and depth. It has *three dimensions.*

> So let's see how we can go about using geometric shapes to enclose some space.

Show the students the examples of each of the sheets.

> What do you notice about each of these? (Press until you get the answers. They are all made up of triangles and squares, they all have sides that are equal in length, and all the angles in the triangles are the same.)

> A triangle that has angles that are all the same is called an **equilateral triangle.** Triangles and squares make strong shape. When the sides are equal they will join together easily, too. There is a name that applies to all these shapes. They are called **regular polyhedra.** That means that they are shapes that have many sides

that are equal. There are **irregular polyhedra** too. What would they be? (Shapes with many sides that are not equal.)

The first geometric enclosed space that you can make out of these geometric shapes is formed by triangles— four of them. When they are put together, the shape will look like this.

Show the example of 1.

Does anyone know what we call this shape. It isn't a **pyramid.** What is different about it? (The base is not a square.)

It is a pretty big word, but it is fun to say. Right. It is a **tetrahedron.** Say it. All right, now you can make one.

Hand out copies of Sheet 1. Let them color all but the tabs, if they wish, and then cut them out.

I am going to give you some instructions for assembling this shape. I think it will help you, if you do each step as I describe it. Have your cutout piece on your desk. Be sure you have enough room to work.

1. Fold each section on the lines toward the center. Make sharp folds and be sure they are right on the line.
2. Fold the tabs toward the middle.
3. Squeeze some glue on a piece of paper. Get a toothpick to spread it with and spread a little glue on the tabs.
4. Carefully bring all the sides together, slip the tabs in the inside, and gently press them together. If all the sides are worked at the same time, your shape will assemble quite easily.

If the children press a little too hard and the shape crushes a little, use the piece of wire to poke inside and pop the sides back out. The wire can be used to help the tabs to stick to the main pieces.

Now it is assembled. What do we call it? Yes, a tetrahedron. After the glue has set, as it has in this sample, you can press your finger gently on the point. (Ask a student to do this on the sample.) How does it feel? Pretty solid? Why? It is made up of triangles so it is **geometrically stable.** Triangles can take a lot of weight and you can't push them around much. If we were going to make a space big enough to get inside, how would a tetrahedron work? Would you have enough room to sit down? Remember the floor is a triangle. How much room would there be for your head? Remember the walls would come together in a point. Would there be a roof?

Let's try another shape that will have a little bigger floor because it will be a square. It will have five pieces—four triangles and the square.

Show the example of 2.

What do we call this one? It is easy to spot a **pyramid,** isn't it? That is partly because it is more familiar to you. After your experience with the tetrahedron, it will probably be easy for you to put it together, too.

Hand out copies of sheet 2. Go through the instructions with them again. When they have completed it, say:

Does it feel about the same when you press down on the point? It is quite solid, or geometrically stable, too, and there is more room on the floor, but what about room for your head?

Let's see how the next one might work.

Show the example of 3.

This one is very familiar to you. What do you call it? (A cube.) It is a cube, but it is also a **polyhedron,** so it is going to have one of those strange names. How many sides does a hexagon have? How many sides does this cube have? Does that give you a clue? Yes, it has something to do with "hex". It is called a **hexahedron.**

Hand out copies of sheet 3. Go through the instructions again. When they have completed the shape, say:

How does the hexahedron feel when you press your finger down on top? Is it as stable as the others? It might need some **reinforcing,** but what advantages does it have as a space to get into? (It has more floor space and more room for your head.)

Some of the students may not be ready to go beyond this point. For younger students, go on to the closure at the end. For older students having trouble assembling the shapes, give them the option of making several of the simpler ones.

Now I think you are ready for a hard one.

Show the example of 4.

Do you have any idea what this is called? It is an **octahedron.** Do these names tell you something about each of the shapes? What do you think the *hedron* part of it means? (The kind of shape it is.) What about *tetra, hexa* and *octa*? (The number of sides it has.)

Have copies of each of the sheets displayed on the wall.

What is the difference between each of these shapes? Count the sides each of them has. Now can you figure out what *tetra* means? (Four sides.) And *hexa*? (Six sides.) And *octa*? (Eight sides.)

Hand out copies of sheet 4. The instructions are similar except make this suggestion.

This shape has more sides and and it will be a little more complicated to put together. Start folding in the middle and work to the outside, as you did with the others. But you might want to start at one end and work to the other end, also.

When they have completed the shape, say:

This polyhedron is made up eight equilateral triangles and no squares. Press your finger on one of the points. What happens? (It is solid enough, but it wants to tip over.) This shape would have to be reinforced too, but not in the same way as the square. After you finish making all the shapes we will do a little experimenting with reinforcement.

There are six different shapes that we have the patterns for and each one is a little harder than the last. Some of you may be ready to try another one.

Show the example of 5a and 5b.

You may be familiar with this one because it is often used for a Christmas ornament. It is an **icosahedron.** It is pretty hard to figure out how many sides it has by looking at it, isn't it? When you try to count around the shape, you lose track of where you started. Let's look at the pattern. It is a pretty one isn't it? How many sides? (20 sides.)

Hand out copies of sheet 5. Work from the center out and from one end to the other as before.

How about this one? What happens to it when you press your finger on it? The floor is just one of the triangles and it is a pretty big space to support on one triangle. If it was big enough to get inside, there wouldn't be much room on the floor. You could lean against the sloping sides a little bit and you *would* have quite a bit of room for your head. But we would have to figure out a way to reinforce or enlarge the base of this one, too, wouldn't we?

Well, if you have made it this far, you can probably manage this last one.

Show the example of 6.

There isn't much chance that you can guess the name of this one! It looks very complicated when you write it. It is a **cuboctahedron.** There are some clues in that word, however, that should help you figure out how many sides it has. Start with the first part *cub*. It is pronounced like cube and how many sides did a cube have? (Six.) The next part is *octa*. How many sides was that? (Eight.) Why do you think they use both terms? What shape were the sides of a cube? (Squares.) And of an octahedron? So what do we have here? (A shape with six squares and eight triangles.) How many sides does that make for this shape then? (Fourteen.)

Hand out two copies of sheet 6 to each student. The instructions are similar except point out that. . .

With the other shapes you were only working with one pattern. On this one you will be cutting out two sheets and putting them together. You will also have paste on the extra piece that wouldn't fit on the sheet.

When the students have finished at least one model of each shape (or several of the simpler shapes if the students are younger or having trouble), comment. . .

When you were assembling these shapes, how would you describe what happened as you brought the sides all together? (It became stronger, more rigid.) When you bring triangles and squares together, they reinforce each other. The squares alone are not as strong as triangles but they become stronger when they are combined with triangles.

Closure

Now you have six (or three) examples of regular polyhedra. Do you have any idea how many of these shapes with many sides with the same dimension and equal angles there are? They weren't easy to put together but it helped when you understood the proces for assembling them. When you worked through the process to assemble one shape you could apply it to the next one. Understanding the process for accomplishing something makes it easier to do a similar thing another time. You don't have to sit around and wonder what to do next!

There are 75 known regular polyhedra. Why do they say 75 "known" polyhedra? That means that there may be more that no one has figured out yet. Maybe you will want to try to invent a new one. They do get pretty complicated when you get to the seventieth or seventy-fifth one, however. And after that there are more things that you can do with geometric shapes by projecting triangles and squares out from the base shape. Mathematics offers endless possibilities.

What is something else that you might say about these shapes? Aren't they pretty? Many things that can be worked out with math turn out to be very beautiful. Look around you the rest of the day and at home tonight and find at least three examples of regular polyhedra that are beautiful to share with us tomorrow.

GEOMETRIC SHAPES FOR ENCLOSING SPACE

SHEET I FORMS A TETRAHEDRON

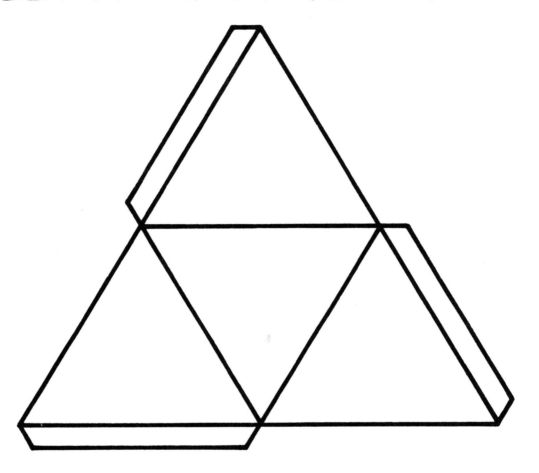

GEOMETRIC SHAPES FOR ENCLOSING SPACE

SHEET 2 FORMS A PYRAMID

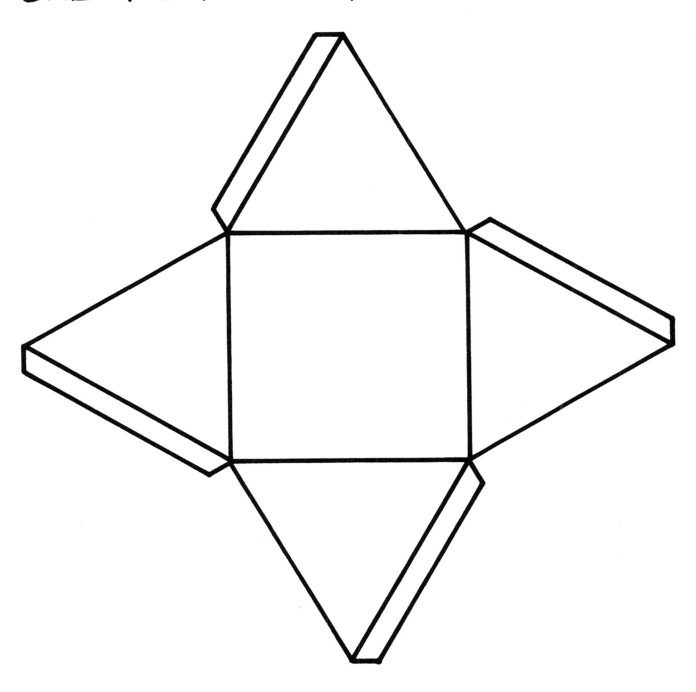

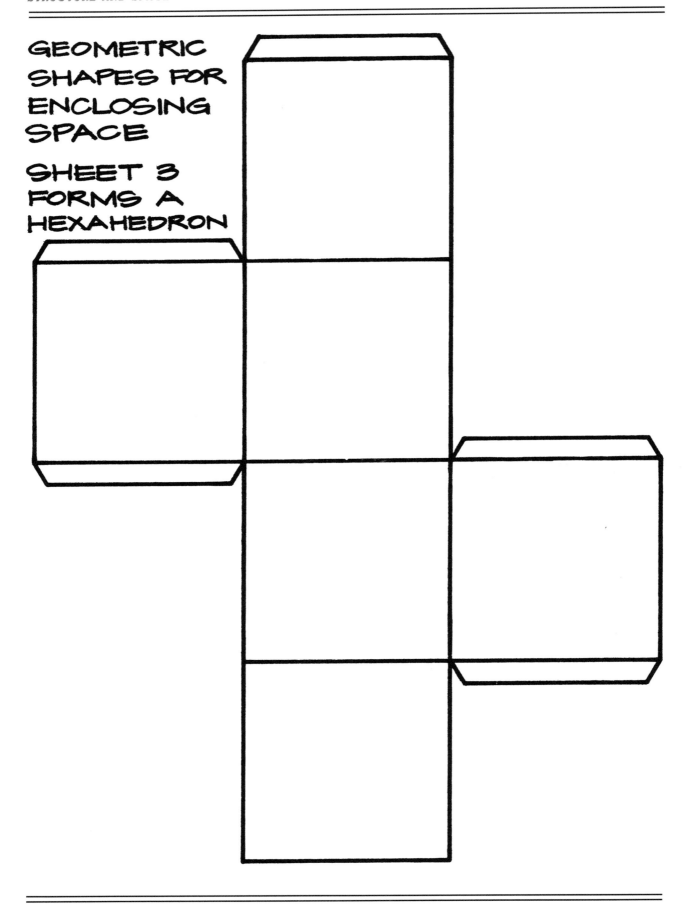

GEOMETRIC
SHAPES FOR
ENCLOSING
SPACE

SHEET 3
FORMS A
HEXAHEDRON

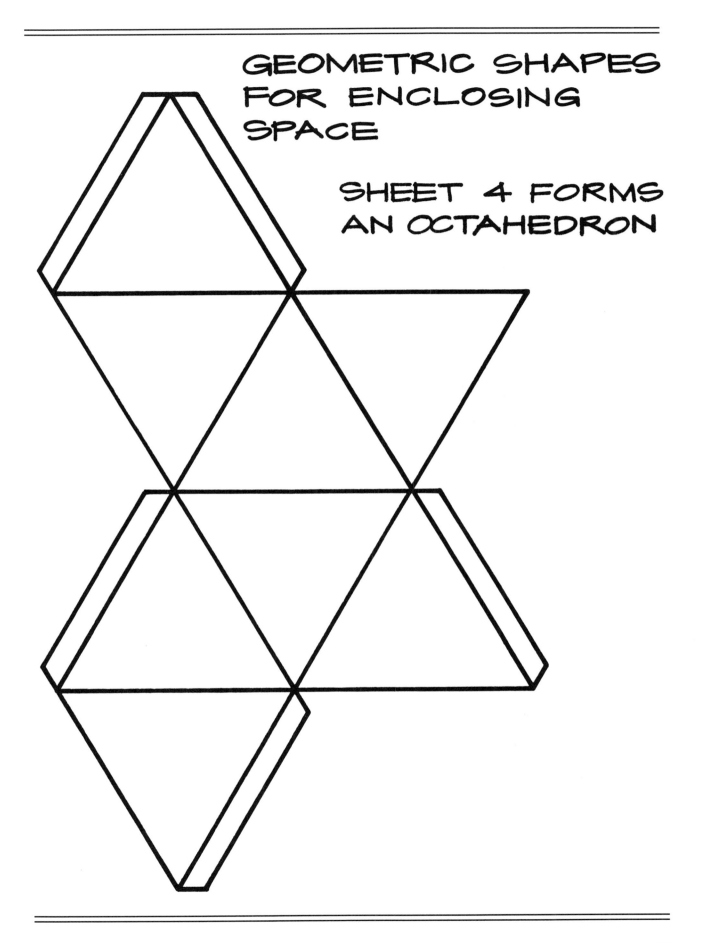

GEOMETRIC SHAPES
FOR ENCLOSING
SPACE

SHEET 4 FORMS
AN OCTAHEDRON

GEOMETRIC SHAPES FOR ENCLOSING SPACE

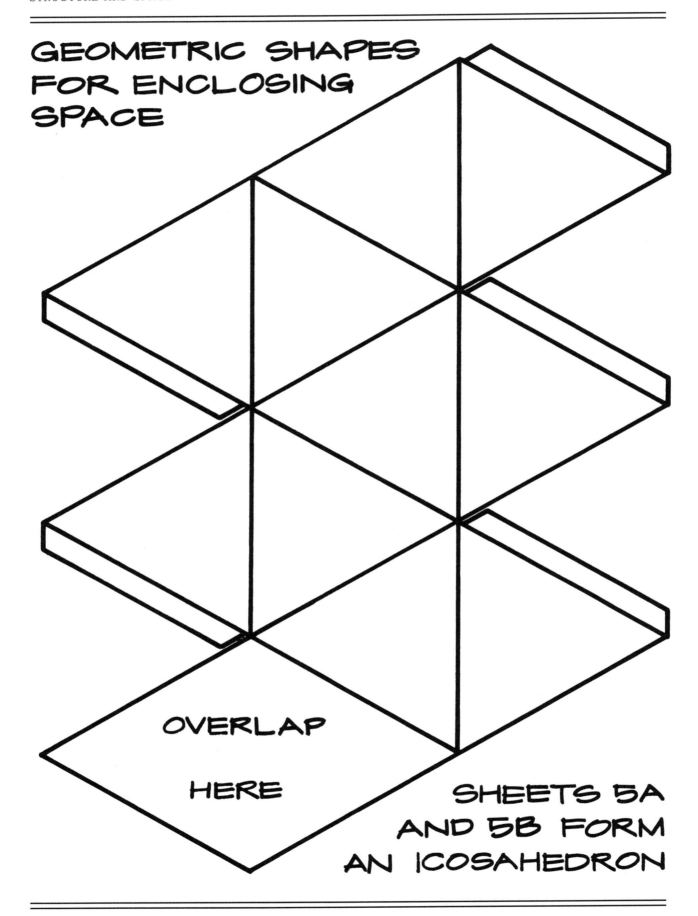

OVERLAP

HERE

SHEETS 5A AND 5B FORM AN ICOSAHEDRON

GEOMETRIC SHAPES FOR ENCLOSING SPACE

PASTE OVER OVERLAP AREA ON SHEET 5A

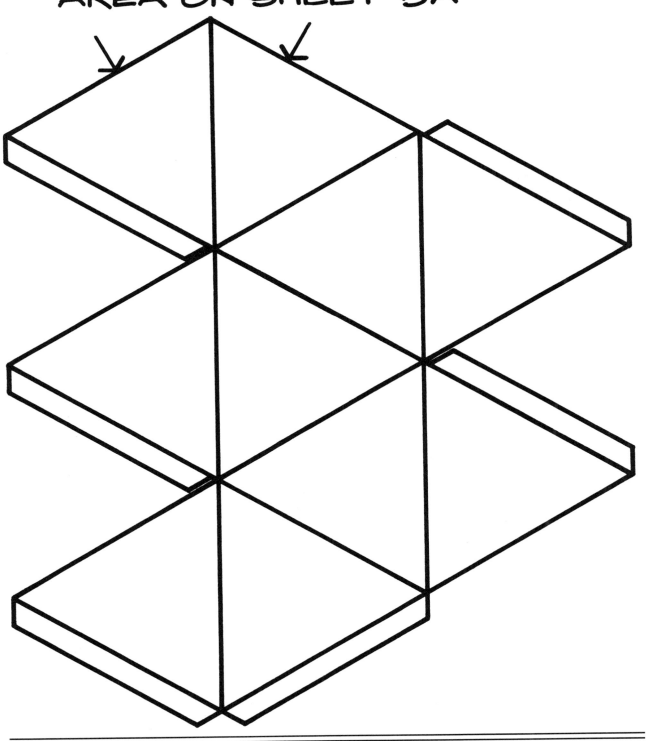

GEOMETRIC SHAPES FOR ENCLOSING SPACE

2 COPIES OF SHEET 6 FORM A CUBOCTA- HEDRON

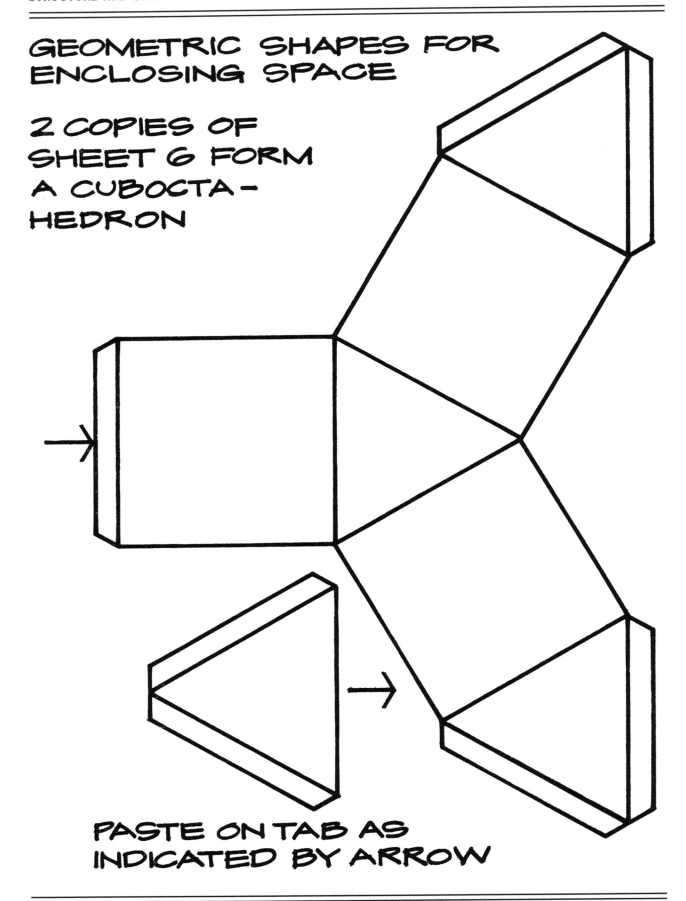

PASTE ON TAB AS INDICATED BY ARROW

CREATING NEW SHAPES FOR ENCLOSING SPACE

Theme

Experiencing the design process by combining models of individual geometric shapes into groupings to provide a model for a classroom reading or "time-out" space increases familiarity with the shapes. Visualizing the interior space, how it will be entered, and what openings to make develops a sense of spatial awareness and of the relationship of spaces to the surrounding area.

Learning Objectives

To understand the use of a process in the development of a product
To appreciate aesthetic qualities in the surroundings through mathematics
To understand the relationship between the establishment and the application of criteria

Subject Matter

Math
Science
Art
Language Arts

Time

Teacher and students forty-five to sixty minutes in the classroom

Vocabulary Words

models   **structure**
designers   **planning**
design criteria **process**
reinforce

Materials

Each student should have general models of regular polyhedra made previously
   Additional copies of patterns for *"Geometric Shapes for Enclosing Space"* for cutting out and assembling more if needed
Scissors
Glue

Toothpicks
A piece of rigid wire
Masking tape

Preparation

Students: Models made in previous session
Teacher: Assembling materials and going over lesson plan

You have made some very pretty **models.** They are nice to have around just to look at, but what else might they be used for? (A mobile, ornament, etc.)

Have you ever put together a model for a car or an airplane? It was a small example of something much bigger, wasn't it? Maybe these shapes could be models for something bigger. Let's think about using them to create a model for a reading or "Time Out" space for our classroom. Do you think you could get in one of these spaces if it was made bigger? (Press for comments about floor space, head room, space to lean against, etc.) Would you want to be in the space alone? If it is going to be big enough for several people, what would you probably want to do with these models? (Join them together.) We can join these shapes together quite easily. Do you remember why? (Because all the edges are equal.)

When you made the models, you had to follow instructions and be very careful and accurate, but now you are going to be something more. You are going to be **designers** of a structure.

If you are going to *design* something that you and your friends will spend some time in, you will need to establish some **design criteria.** That means thinking about some of the things that need to be included in the design, if it is going to meet the needs of those who will use it. What would some of those things be?

Encourage thinking about such things as:

Who will use it?
How many will use it at one time?
How will it be used?
How much floor space will be needed?
Will there be room for everyone's head?
How will the space be entered?
Will it need furniture, pillows?

As they make decisions list the design criteria on a chart.

You have developed some design criteria and you have some very beautiful shapes to work with. Now, it is time to get started on the project. Joining the shapes together will give you a chance to be very creative. There are so many possibilities. Try out as many ideas as you possibly can before you decide on your final design. Using the masking tape to put them together temporarily allows you to make changes. Move the pieces around as you think of other possibilities to try out.

You may want to suggest that the children work in pairs if they wish. Working together is more stimulating for some and they will have more shapes to work with. As they work, comment on good ideas as they emerge and pose questions relating to the criteria. After about half an hour, ask for the students' attention and initiate a discussion about openings.

In addition to having an entrance to your **structure** you are probably going to want some light and to be able to see out. You will also want to get from one section of the structure to another. We will need some more design criteria.

Where should the openings be?

How should the openings be cut so the walls won't fall down?

When you were making the models, what happened as you brought all the sides together? (The whole shape became stronger.) What will happen when you join several shapes together then? They will **reinforce** each other and make the whole structure stronger. That will make it possible to cut out areas for openings in some of the walls without collapsing the whole structure. In fact, you may also leave one or two walls out entirely, if there are other walls around them for support.

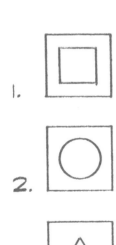

Here are three possible shapes for openings. (Draw them on the criteria chart.) Which one of these would be the weakest? (The square, because it removes the most material.) Why is 3 the strongest? One reason is because a triangle is stronger, but take a good look. What is another reason? The square removes the most area from the flat shape, the circle is next, but the triangle removes the least area and therefore weakens it the least. However, it also gives you the least room to look out or go through. You could solve the problem by making the square smaller. You might find it more interesting to combine smaller openings. These are choices you will need to make. Which openings you choose will depend on what the opening is to be used for and how strong the surrounding walls are. You will need to be careful not to have too many openings.

1.

2.

3.

When you have thought it over carefully and have decided where to *design* your openings you can draw them on your model. If you are going to leave a whole section out, draw an X on it. **Planning** your design on the model will make the full size structure more stable and more pleasing to look at.

Fifteen minutes before the session is to end, have them put all their creations on a table. Conduct a discussion about how they have met the design criteria. Have them decide which one would be the best design for a full-size structure for the classroom. You may want to encourage a combination of the designs.

You have selected a design that can be built and should make a very nice classroom space.

Closure

Put up a chart and initiate a discussion on what has been done in this activity. Press for answers such as: assembled materials, determined design criteria, applied the criteria to a design project, made a model, analyzed the design, or made a group decision on the final design.

You have gone through the steps of a **process.** Let's see if you can tell me what the steps in that process were.

Now that you know what the process is, you could use it anytime you have an idea about something you know how to put it in a form that people can see. When people understand what you plan to do, they will help you make or build something. Having a process for doing something is a very useful tool.

BUILDING A "TIME-OUT" SPACE

Theme

Constructing a full-size structure from a model of the design illustrates the principles of scale, proportion, and strength. It also reinforces the need for accuracy and develops a sense of the relationship between the human body and the space it occupies.

Learning Objectives

To understand the relationship between measurement, scale, and proportion
To gain motor skills while implementing a process
To gain ability in working together in a group to
understand criteria for the use of tools

Subject Matter

Math
Science
Art

Time

Teacher: Call ahead to an appliance store or other source to arrange for cardboard cartons and pick up.
One-half hour to cut cartons apart
Call one or two parents to help in the classroom to cut cartons.
Students: One 45- to 60-minute class period to cut the shapes, measure, and drill. Extra time for small groups to paint and assemble.

Vocabulary Words

dimensions
regular polyhedra
design criteria
structure
space
model
pattern

Materials

Four or five large corrugated cardboard cartons. Appliance stores have a good supply, or large blueprint companies have nice flat ones from paper supplies; and 4' × 8' sheets of double corrugated cardboard are available for purchase from cardboard box companies.

Utility knives

Punch or electric drill

Yardsticks, rulers, and pencils

See instructions for handling on page 188–189.

Water-base paint and brushes: cheap sponge brushes come in various widths and speed the painting. They can be thrown away.

Garden twine that is heavy but soft (comes in colors). Nylon twine stretches too much and the structure cannot be tightened up sufficiently.

Masking tape

Duct tape, if you are not going to do lacing. (Masking or cellophane tapes do not work.)

Preparation

Cut the cardboard cartons apart and remove excess, so that there is a supply of large, flat sheets. Save some strips for reinforcing.

Decide whether to use lacing or duct tape for fastening the structure together. Duct tape makes a much more solid structure but it is so sticky that it is hard for students to handle. Probably students in the sixth grade and up could work with it well. You would have to do the taping for younger students.

Getting parent help makes the project go more quickly and smoothly and provides supervision while students experience using tools.

A small (12-inch) model of a shape laced together would help you understand how the lacing works and help the students to see what they are going to be doing.

Procedure

You have selected a design for our **structure** and we have this nice **model** of it. How can we use this model to make something bigger and be sure that it comes out looking just the same? (You need to measure the size of the model, then decide how big you want the structure to be.)

When we talk about measurements like these, we are talking about dimensions. The dimensions will include how long, how high, and how wide the structure is. We developed this design by using **regular polyhedra.** What dimension do regular polyhedra have in common? (All the edges are the same length.) That certainly makes it easy. If all the edges are the same length, they should fit together very well and you will have only one **dimension** to think about.

But, since all the edges have to fit together, what do we need to be concerned about when we measure that one dimension on each edge? (That all the measurements are accurate so each edge is the same.)

What might happen if different people were measuring edges and some people were more accurate than others (The edges wouldn't match.) Then our structure wouldn't look like the model, would it? How could we solve that problem?

Why did our models turn out so well? (They were made from patterns.) So, if we make a **pattern** and everyone is very careful about tracing around it, then all the edges should match. How many different flat shapes do we have? (Two—a square and a triangle.)

How many patterns will we need?

Now we have to do some thinking. How will we know how big to make the patterns? We will have to decide how big the structure is to be. How can we determine that? We will need to decide on some **design criteria.** If this is to be a quiet reading space, what the design criteria be? (Not too many people in it at a time, and that they are comfortable.) If the structure is to be in the room for some time, what else would we need to think about? (The space available in the room.)

Let's do a little experimenting to see if we can figure out the right size. Let's use this table as a start.

Have three or four students get under the table and simulate stretching out, reading a book, and playing a game.

Do you feel as though you have enough room? Remember we want this **space** to be comfortable and cozy for you. Do you need all the space? Is there enough head room? We could make some parts of it higher like your model, couldn't we?

A table is usually 30 inches high so this works well as a demonstration. It will limit the maximum size of a shape to 30 inches, which is about the maximum size the cardboard cartons will allow.

Take a yardstick and measure the space you have decided on. You will need dimensions for the height, width, and length. One of you measure, another check, and another write them down. Now we have the approximate dimensions for our structure. What else do we need to think about? Take a look at our material.

Can we get the pieces out of the cardboard? Better measure it. Thirty inches is about the largest dimension we can get out of our cartons. It looks like 30 inches maximum will be a good size to meet all of our design criteria.

Take another look at our material. Why will this be a good building material? Look at the edge. What is inside? The corrugations are sort of like triangles reinforcing the paper, aren't they? That makes material much stronger.

Have the students make patterns for a 30-inch square and a 30-inch equilateral triangle. (See Useful Tools for how to cut.) For younger students the patterns could be provided.)

Look at your model. How many triangles will you need? How many squares?

Make a note of each number of the chart. If the model has fewer pieces than the number of pairs in the class, let the students cut extra pieces. They will probably be added on at the end. Divide the class in pairs.

One of you must hold the pattern very firmly on the cardboard so that it doesn't move, as the other traces around all the edges. If your line isn't too straight, even it up with the yardstick, then you will be ready to cut it out.

Even younger students can manage quite well with utility knives, if they are well instructed and supervised. See page 188 for a checklist of cautions for using their knives.

As with all tools, there are tricks that provide good results. When cutting corrugated cardboard with utility knives:

1. On the first cut only press hard enough to go through the first layer of paper. If you press too hard, you won't be able to stay right on the line.
2. Make two or three more runs down the line going a little deeper each time until you are all the way through.
3. Press the knife into each side of the corners to cut them clear through.

When you have finished cutting out your piece, you will need to measure and mark the location of the holes for the laces. This should be done very carefully and accurately. The holes should be one inch in from the edge so they won't pull out. Find one inch on your ruler. One of you hold the ruler while the other marks the one-inch point at three different places along the

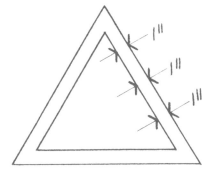

HOLES
EVERY 2"

edge. One of you hold a yardstick very tight along the three marks while the other draws a line through the marks. Do the same thing for each of the edges.

When all the lines are drawn one of you should hold a yardstick or ruler almost on the line while the other places marks that cross through the line every two inches. That is so you will know exactly where to drill the hole. Start the first mark at the place where the lines intersect near the corner and measure from that point, not from the very edge. If you have measured correctly, on an edge that is 30 inches long, you should have 15 marks. The ones at the corners will be common to both sides.

Using an electric drill is recommended because it is faster and does a better job. It is also an excellent opportunity to reinforce the concept of girls being just as capable with power tools as boys.

Have the drill ready to use with a 1/4-inch or 3/8-inch bit. Putting the cardboard piece over a wastebasket works very well for drilling. Have a scrap piece of cardboard for practice first. The drill will kick back a little but the students learn to compensate for that. Running the motor while pulling back out makes it easier.

Now we are going to drill the holes for the laces. You will need to support the body of the drill with one hand while you point the drill straight above the mark for the hole. You don't need to press very hard. The motor will do the work for you.

Give all the students a chance to experience drilling.

Our pieces are ready to be painted now so we have another decision to make. What colors do you want for your structure?

Put out the available water-base paint and let them choose a combination of four or five colors. Select a place for the painting. Outside on the grass is nice in good weather and if there is supervisory help.

Put each color in a container such as coffee can and assign the brushes. The sponge brushes cover the surface quickly. They also can give a nice effect when two students work with two compatible colors and start at each side, working toward the center. When they get near the center they can blend the colors by each brushing over the area.

The shapes should be painted on both sides.

The next step is for the students to select the lacings. Having two or three colors again allows the opportunity for choice.

Wrap the ends of the laces very tightly with masking tape so they will go through the holes easily. Have the students work together, one holding while the other laces. Cut the lacing pieces plenty long so there will be extra length at each end for pulling the laces tight and tying the ends.

Following the model, lace the pieces into pairs first. Then start joining them together in larger groupings. The final lacing will require someone inside and out, one pushing the lace in and the other catching it and pushing it back through the next hole.

When all the pieces are laced loosely into place, students can start tightening the structure up. Check each one before they tie it to be sure it has been pulled tight all along the edge. Tie one corner, then re-tighten to the opposite corner before tying it. It may be necessary to re-tighten corners as others are tied and the structure becomes more rigid.

With lacing the structure will always be a little wobbly and it may be necessary to add a few bracing strips, particularly around the entrance opening.

Closure

Building this space is quite an accomplishment. It was a lot of hard work but we did some things that made it easier. What were some things we did that made it easier? (We planned the design ahead of time, had a model to follow, had a process for measuring, and had some tools and techniques to help us.) Any project will turn out better if each step is thought through before starting and when everyone works together to get the project done.

THOUGHTS ABOUT A SPACE

Theme

Spaces are being experienced so constantly, and in rapid succession, that often there is little awareness of the effect they are having on personal feelings and ability to function. Focusing thoughts on a space increases sensitivity to the everyday environment.

Learning Objectives

To increase language skills by focusing on some words and their usage
To provide a format for creative writing
To increase sensitivity to the daily environment

Subject Matter

Language Arts
Science

Time

One 45- to 60-minute classroom session

Vocabulary Words

Brainstorming

Materials

Copies of the sheet "Inner Space Poem"
Pencils or pens

Preparation

While the activity could be done in relation to many things, it is planned as a follow-up to the activity Building a "Time-Out" Space. Prior to this activity the students should have had ample time to use the "time-out" space or to experience some other space.

Procedure

You have worked so hard on building your **space structure** and you have spent some time in it. Now let's try to put some of your thoughts into a kind of poem. You won't find this kind of poem in any poetry books because it is a special poem just for your project. It is called an "Innter Space Poem" and there are two reasons for that. Can you figure out what they are?

Show the hand-out sheet.

It is going to be about an inner space and it is going to fit into a space.

There are going to be some special rules about this poem, also. You will notice that there is just one space at the top and at the bottom. Those spaces are for your secret words.

The other three lines have more words and we are going to do a little **brainstorming** on those so you will have a lot of words to choose from.

Make three headings across the chalkboard so that the words in each category can be listed as the students mention them.

2
TRIANGULAR
STRANGE
COLORFUL

3
LACED
MEASURED
PAINTED

4
COZY
CLOSED IN
NICE

The second line has two spaces and they will be for adjectives that describe this space.

Keep encouraging the students to come up with words until there are between 20 and 30 in the column.

The third line has three spaces and they are to be for *verbs* that tell what you did while making the structure.

The fourth line has two spaces again and they will be for *adjectives* also, but this time they will describe how the space makes you feel.

Hand out the sheets and ask the students to follow along with you while writing in the words.

1. On the first line, write your secret name for this space. Don't say it out loud. Keep it a secret until the end.

2. On line two write in two adjectives that describe this space. You may use the list that we have made or you may have thought of another one. Remember that you are writing a poem so you will want the words to go together well.
3. On line three write three verbs that tell what you did when you made the structure. Again use the words on the list or think of others. Make them go nicely with the adjectives in line two. You may want some of them to rhyme.
4. On line four write two adjectives that describe how the space makes you feel.

When the students have finished ask them to read their poems aloud, or if they are inclined to be shy, collect them and give an expressive reading yourself.

Closure

Those were interesting "Inner Space Poems." It was fun to do them but it also helped you to really think about the qualities of the space and how you felt about being in it. We don't realize how much spaces effect us. Quite often we act in a certain way because of the space we are in.

There are spaces we go into that make us feel we shouldn't talk. Others make us want to run and shout. Sometimes we feel cross and irritated and we don't realize that it is because the space we are in is too crowded, too hot, or too noisy. Sometimes we feel good and are not aware that it is because the space we are in is comfortable, has nice colors, or is a beautiful space.

Look for spaces that make you feel irritated, and ones that make you feel good and tell us about it tomorrow or write a poem about it.

Tomorrow we will read some of the poems and compare your feelings and descriptions.

INNER SPACE POEM

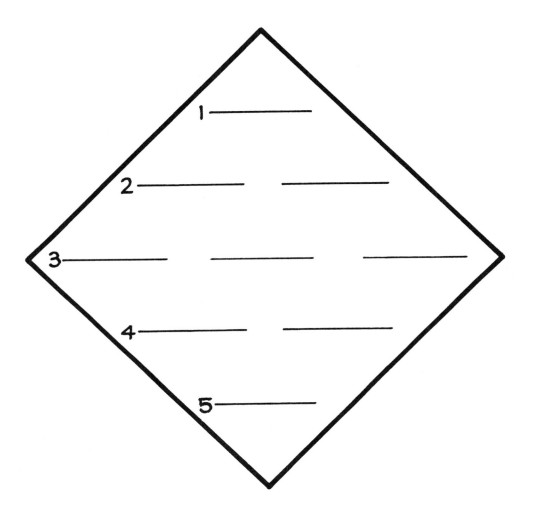

5 USEFUL TOOLS AND TECHNIQUES

INTRODUCTION

Theme

While these tools and techniques may already be familiar to teachers and students, learning about the manner in which they are used by architects and others trained in design and drafting techniques can be both interesting and useful.

By way of introduction to the use of any of these tools and techniques in the series of activities, it would be an excellent idea to invite an architect or other design professional to the classroom to discuss the use of the tools and to demonstrate the techniques. After this initial introduction, the architect could be asked to come in to the classroom a time or two to help the students to use them in their activity projects.

An architect can be found by contacting the nearest chapter of the American Institute of Architects, writing the national headquarters of the American Institute of Architects, 1735 New York Avenue, Washington, D.C. 20006, or calling an architect listed in the yellow pages of the telephone director. Most architects will be very cooperative when the purpose is explained, so try again if the first call is not productive.

Tools and Techniques

1. Pacing for Measuring Large Areas
2. Rulers at Various Scales
3. Laying out a Grid
4. Drafting a Drawing
5. Utility Knives and Electric Drills Needn't Be Dangerous
6. Charts for Recording a Process
7. Clipboards for Status
8. Environmental Planning Vocabulary List

PACING FOR MEASURING LARGE AREAS

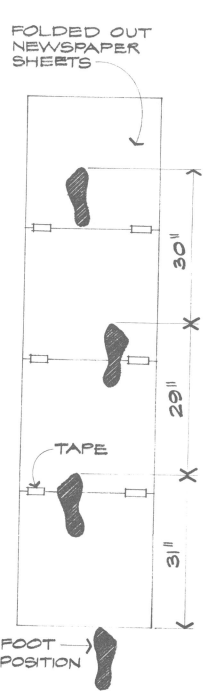

FOLDED OUT NEWSPAPER SHEETS

30"

29"

TAPE

31"

FOOT POSITION

Time

Forty-five to sixty minutes

Materials

Newspapers
Masking tape
Felt pens
Yardstick

Pacing is a very useful tool for making field measurements of large areas. With a little practice adults are able to establish a reliable pace in which each comfortable stride will equal about 3 feet. Architects and surveyors often use the pace for measuring large areas. The variations in body size of elementary students will have more effect on the size of the pace than it does with adults, so they need to establish their own individual pace.

Directions for Step 1

Fold out four or five pieces of newspaper and tape the short sides together.

With the toe at the beginning edge of the paper, the pacer should take three long but easy, rhythmic strides across the paper. It is a good idea to practice a little.

Another student should record the position of the toe at each pace with a felt market. This must be done quickly so the rhythm of the pace is not lost.

The pacer then uses the yardstick to measure the distance between the marks and should write the three measurements down in a column.

The process should be repeated three times so that a reasonably accurate average can be obtained.

Directions for Step 2

The pacer now has three columns of three figures. These figures should look something like those shown on page 181.

Divide each of these answers by three to obtain the average pace for each of the groups of figures.

Add the three answers together.

Divide again by three to obtain the pace. Round the figure off. The result will be a quite reliable average pace.

With a little practice and concentration the individual will be able to measure the classroom areas with acceptable accuracy. Students will have experienced a realistic application of mathematics.

The pace can be used for many types of mapping projects or for measuring a house and drawing its floor plan.

$$
\begin{array}{r} 31 \\ 29 \\ 30 \\ \hline 90 \end{array}
\qquad
\begin{array}{r} 32 \\ 28 \\ 31 \\ \hline 91 \end{array}
\qquad
\begin{array}{r} 31 \\ 29 \\ 28 \\ \hline 88 \end{array}
$$

$$
\begin{array}{r} 30 \\ 3\overline{)90} \\ 9 \\ \hline \end{array}
\qquad
\begin{array}{r} 30.3 \\ 3\overline{)91} \\ 9 \\ \hline 10 \\ 9 \\ \hline 1 \end{array}
\qquad
\begin{array}{r} 29.3 \\ 3\overline{)88} \\ 6 \\ \hline 28 \\ 27 \\ \hline 1 \end{array}
$$

$$
\begin{array}{r} 30 \\ 30.3 \\ 29.3 \\ \hline 89.6 \end{array}
\qquad
\begin{array}{r} 29.86 \\ 3\overline{)89.6} \\ 6 \\ \hline 29 \\ 27 \\ \hline 26 \\ 24 \\ \hline 2 \end{array}
\qquad
30'' \ PACE
$$

RULERS AT VARIOUS SCALES

Theme

First experiences in drawing in scale are usually quite confusing for the student. There are so many marks on the standard ruler that students have trouble keeping them straight. The rulers shown in the example sheet will make it easier to work in these three most commonly used scales.

The six-inch ruler is often used by architects and engineers because it is easier to handle when drawing details on a scale drawing.

Activity

Cut the rulers out and glue them to strips of light-weight cardboard.

Using graph paper in the selected scale is also recommended for beginners. It is an aid in laying out the measurements and in keeping the lines straight and parallel.

Encourage the students to use the rulers, however, rather than counting the squares. For instance, measuring twenty feet at a scale of ½ in. = 1 ft. 0 in. can be done more quickly with the ruler than by counting the squares.

To become accustomed to drawing in scale, ask the students to lay out a 10'0" × 12'0" room and a 9'6" × 13'6" room in each of the three scales using the proper ruler.

The goal is to develop the ability to use and understand the markings on a standard ruler by practicing with the simplified versions. Encourage the students to switch to the standard ruler as soon as they feel comfortable with the markings.

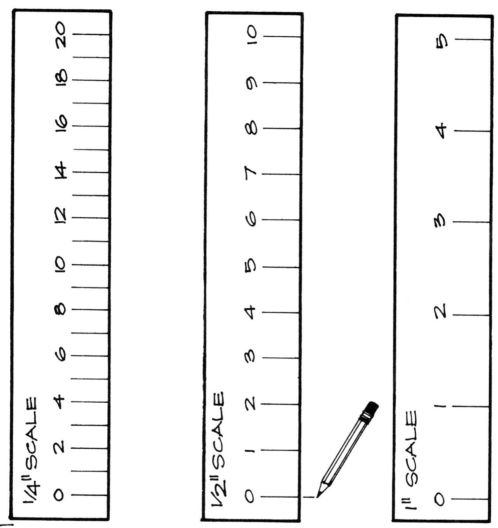

NOTE: PENCIL SHOULD BE SHARP.
MAKE MARKS ON SAME SIDE AS RULER MARKS.
MAKE MARKS IN SAME DIRECTION AS RULER MARKS.

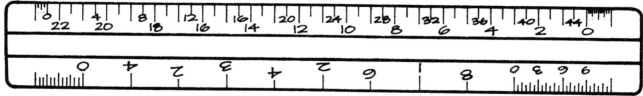

ARCHITECT'S SCALE

LAYING OUT A GRID

Theme

Any drawing, map, photograph, poster, etc., can easily be reduced or enlarged by the use of a grid, which is a series of carefully measured lines forming a network of squares over the piece being worked with.

1. The ability to measure accurately.
2. The ability to observe detail.
3. The ability to recognize the differences resulting from the use of different scales.

Activity

Overlay the piece being copied with a series of horizontal and vertical lines that form squares. It will be easier if the measurement is an even one such as one, two, four, or ten inches. If a specific area is to be filled by drawing, then it may be necessary to divide the size of the space by the number of squares in the grid overlay and an uneven number may result.

The size of the squares will depend not only on the size of the space to be filled but also on the size of the piece being worked with and the amount of detail it contains. If there is a great deal of detail the grid needs to be smaller.

It will be important to keep the lines parallel to one another and horizontal lines perpendicular to the vertical ones. This provides excellent practice in accurate measurement.

Sheets 1 and 2 will give the students a process for laying out the grid. It would be helpful to complete the drawing on the example sheet just to get the idea.

When starting to draw after the grid has been laid out, encourage the students to draw lightly at first so they can make corrections. They should start at one corner and very carefully observe just where the lines go in each square so they can put them in exactly the same place in the new square.

Putting in the larger forms first gets the whole picture in scale, which is a good idea to use to avoid having to make too many corrections as the details are filled in.

This process takes concentration and judgment.

The grid technique is useful in making displays, presentations, and in developing graphics for floors, walls, or ceilings.

HOW TO USE A GRID FOR ENLARGING OR REDUCING A DRAWING OR PICTURE

SHEET 1

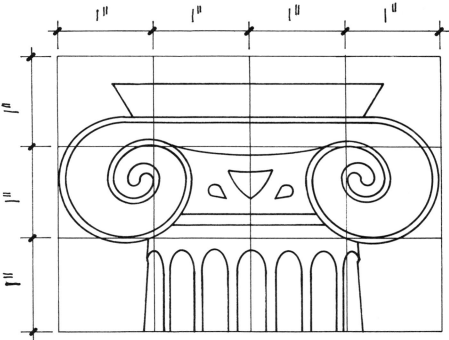

½" SCALE

NOTE: THE LARGER DRAWING IS TWO TIMES THE SIZE OF THE SMALLER ONE.

1" SCALE

NOTE: TO ENLARGE A DRAWING TO FIT A PARTICULAR SPACE, MEASURE THE SPACE AND DIVIDE BY THE NUMBER OF SQUARES IN THE GRID.

THE SPACE FOR THE GRID ON SHEET 2 IS 6". BY DIVIDING 6" BY 4 GRID SPACES, A DIMENSION OF 1½" RESULTS.

BY CAREFULLY OBSERVING THE 1" SCALE DRAWING, COMPLETE THE DRAWING ON SHEET 2.

HOW TO USE A GRID FOR ENLARGING OR REDUCING A DRAWING OR PICTURE

SHEET 2

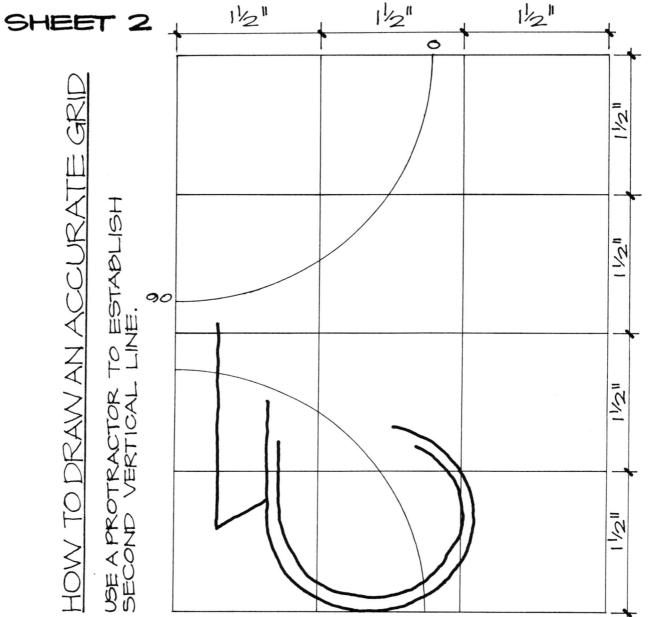

1½"   1½"   1½"

1½"   1½"   1½"   1½"

0

90

HOW TO DRAW AN ACCURATE GRID

USE A PROTRACTOR TO ESTABLISH SECOND VERTICAL LINE.

NOTE: DRAW FIRST HORIZONAL LINE WITH A RULER.

USE A PROTRACTOR TO ESTABLISH SECOND HORIZONTAL LINE.

MARK MEASUREMENTS IN SAME DIRECTION LINE IS TO BE DRAWN.

MARK TWO MEASUREMENTS FOR EACH LINE AND LAY RULER ALONG BOTH WHEN DRAWING THE LINE.

DRAFTING A DRAWING

Theme

Exposing students to the techniques and terminology used in professional drafting of measured drawings provides them with a tool that can be used in many ways. It is also an excellent exposure to a career opportunity with a wide scope of entry levels that can be valuable.

The preparation of measured scale drawings which utilize a standard set of symbols and drawing methods is called *drafting*. Architects, engineers, and a wide variety of industries use people trained in drafting techniques.

The suggestions given here provide a simple beginning for the utilization of drafting techniques in the presentation of ideas that the students develop.

Activity 1

The creative process involves putting ideas in a visual form on paper so they can be studied, experimented with, and changed before a final decision is made.

Students have a tendency to be heavy handed with a pencil. Encourage them to do all their drawing lightly at first so that changes can be easily made as they work without damaging the final appearance of the drawing.

After students have worked with their solution and feel that they have it the way they want it, they can go over the final drawing and "hardline" it in.

Activity 2

If an idea for making some change in an environment is to be actually carried out, the design will need to be presented in an accurate and complete drawing. These are called *working drawings*. They are drawn to a carefully measured scale so that the designs will fit the available space when executed and that all the parts will fit together in a construction.

Because people from many different backgrounds look at plans, there are standard ways for showing things on working drawings. There are ways to show measurements, scale, direction, roads, trees, planting, parking areas, etc. There are also ways to show walls, doors, windows, counters, furniture, etc.

The sheet "Architectural Graphic Standards" illustrates some of the ones that students might be most likely to use. If the students need more information, the book of standards officially approved by the American Institute of Architects is titled *Architectural Graphic Standards* by Ramsey and Sleeper (Wiley).

UTILITY KNIVES AND ELECTRIC DRILLS

Theme

Even younger students can manage quite well with utility knives and electric drills when they are well instructed and supervised.

Using these tools builds confidence in the student in motor skills and develops reliability.

Using these tools also provides an excellent opportunity to demonstrate the girls as well as boys are very capable of using sharp or power driven tools.

Activity 1

Utility knives are very sharp. The check list for the use of the knives should be discussed each time they are used.

Checklist for using utility knives:
1. Never wave the knife or play around with it. Use it only for the execution of the project.
2. Never cut without a large scrap piece of cardboard under the piece that you are cutting out. You can ruin a table top or carpet very easily.
3. Be sure that your other hand and the rest of your body are not in the cutting line. Always look before you cut.
4. Work with a partner. One person should be watching for potential danger while the other works.

Activity 2

As with all tools, there are tricks that provide good results. Here are some tricks for cutting corrugated cardboard with utility knives. Knowing how to cut corrugated cardboard is a good skill to develop because it is a material that is readily available at no cost, it cuts easily, and the edges have enough surface to hold together with glue. It is also heavy enough for structures that are held together with cloth tape or lacing.

Tricks when using utility knives:
1. On the first cut press only hard enough to go through the first layer of the outside paper. If you press too hard, you won't be able to stay on your pencil line and keep the cut straight. This first cut establishes a groove that makes the next ones much easier.
2. Make two or three more runs down the line going a little deeper each time until you are all the way through.

3. Press the point of the knife into each side of a corner to cut them clear through.
4. When you have finished a cut, pull the knife back into its holder so the blade won't be damaged or damage anyone.
5. Change the blade when it becomes a little dull. Tools must be in good condition to do a job well.

Activity 3

Using an electric drill is a fast way to make holes when assembling cardboard or wood structures and is an excellent introduction to the use of power tools. Holes can be used for putting the materials together by lacing, tying, wiring, pegging, etc.

Tricks when using an electric drill:
1. Marking the locations of the holes by measuring carefully and accurately is important for preparation. Consideration will need to be given to how large the hole should be depending on how it is to be used, how far apart the holes should be, and how far from the edge of the material.
2. The size of the drill bit to be used should be determined in relation to the size of the material it is to receive.
3. Getting used to holding the drill properly is necessary. One hand should hold the body of the tool firmly directly above and perpendicular to the spot to be drilled. It is not necessary to press hard, the motor will do the work.
4. Practice using the drill on scrap material first. The drill will kick back a little but students will quickly learn to compensate for that.
5. Running the motor as you pull the drill back out makes it easier and does not damage the hole.
6. Rotate turns often. Each student should do just a few holes at a time. Efficiency with any tool decreases rapidly when arms become tired.
7. Do not hand the drill to the next person. Lay it down for them to pick up.
8. Unplug the drill immediately when finished.
9. Remove the bit and return it to the case.

CHARTS FOR RECORDING A PROCESS

Theme

Often classroom lessons are self-contained. When they are completed, that learning experience ends and the student moves on to something else.

Because this environmental study demonstrates the utilization of processes for the accomplishment of goals that the students and teacher have established, the student should be reminded of the steps that have been part of the process experienced.

Activity

Using large sheets of paper to report information, instructions, and ideas that result from class discussions, rather than writing them on the often erased chalkboard, will provide an on-going record of the process they have utilized.

Reviewing the charts at the end of a series of activities reinforces the steps experienced in the process and their relationship to the achieving of environmental change.

CLIPBOARDS FOR STATUS

Theme

Any walk, even just from the classroom to the cafeteria, can be made an environmental analysis, date-gathering or surveying activity.

A feeling of official status results from giving a student a sheet with spaces provided for filling in specific information and a clipboard on which to write.

Activity

Typical Masonite clipboards are heavy, noisy, and expensive. A box of light-weight cardboard bakery cakeboards equipped with two paper clips make inexpensive clipboards with a very good writing surface due to the wax finish.

If the budget is really tight, the cardboard can be cut on a paper cutter from heavy cardboard boxes or appliance cartons.

ENVIRONMENTAL PLANNING VOCABULARY LIST

Theme

We have emphasized some of the words in these activities to indicate that they are words commonly used in relation to architecture, planning, and environmental awareness. Most of them are quite familiar but the particular meaning may be a little different when used in this context.

Since the goal of this series of activities is to give students the motivation and procedures for becoming citizen participants in creating and implementing environmental change, being able to use and understand these words in their particular sense will be important.

The words listed here are defined in language that a student can understand and might use when discussing the things that have been learned with friends and family.

Vocabulary

aesthetic   having a sense of what is beautiful.

apartment   a place to live that is one of several in a building. The building may be small or may be a high rise.

arch   one-half of a circle. An arch is used a great deal both on the inside and outside of the buildings. It is a structural member that can hold up parts of a building. The Romans are credited with developing the arch.

arcade   a series of arches are joined together in a row.

architect   a person who has graduated from a college or university that offers a degree in architecture, has served a three-year apprenticeship in an architect's office, and has passed an examination given by the state. When people meet all these requirements they are registered architects and may use the word *architect* after their name.

architecture   the building of any kind of space or structure can be called architecture whether it is designed by architects or not. A famous American architect named Frank Lloyd Wright has given us a special definition of architecture as architects see it. "Man first created space in which to live—not only for protection from the elements but protection from fellow man as well. But that was not enough—he meant to make these spaces beautiful. Then was architecture born."

asymetrical   not equally balanced; off center.

awareness   watchful, consciousness, being informed.

balance in design, a condition in which the elements are of equal importance. In structures, a condition in which the load is distributed over the member equally so that it will not tip over or fall off.

beam a horizontal structural member which is held up by vertical supports and which carries a floor, wall, or roof load.

brainstorming stretching the thinking about a subject to get all the ideas about it that you can think of.

cantilever A part of a beam or building that projects out beyond the support.

capital the top part of a post of column.

character all of the qualities that distinguish something; the special sense of a place, building, or work of art.

checklist items listed together for comparison or so that nothing will be overlooked.

citizen participation members of the community becoming informed and involved in decision-making about a proposal or issue.

closed space a space surrounded by walls, buildings, or some other barrier that requires some sort of invitation to enter.

colonnade a series of columns set at regular intervals.

column a post or pillar—usually a support for a beam or an arch.

composition the combining of parts or elements to form a whole.

comprehensive plan a plan that is broad in scope and that is both verbal and visual.

compressed pressed together.

concentrated load bearing down at one point.

conservation preservation; care in the use of resources.

construction building by putting parts together.

contractor a person who furnishes building supplies and performs work for an agreed price.

Corinthian a column with a bell-shaped capital of acanthus leaves; one of the classic Greek orders.

creative involvement contributing in an imaginative, original, and productive way.

critique to discuss merits and faults.

cuboctahedron a 14-sided, three-dimensional geometric shape made up of 6 squares and 8 triangles.

decision-making process making up one's mind to act based on research, observation, and discussion.

deflection the amount a beam bends down from a level line due to weight or distance between supports.

density the number of people or buildings in relation to the size of the area.

design sketches, plans, and drawings done artistically skillfully.

design process the steps involved in designing something which include: finding out what is to be designed, for whom, and for what purpose; proposing a number of solutions; deciding on the final form; developing the solution; and implementing the construction or production.

details drawings of the specific physical characteristics of a design.

dimension the length, width, and height of rooms or objects.

dome a shape similar to one half of a ball made up of a series of arches or triangles joined together.

Doric a column with a boxlike capital; the simplest of the three classic Greek orders.

duplex a house for two families.

established refers to an area or neighborhood that has functioned well for a time and is not always changing.

equilateral triangle a three-sided shape with equal angles and length of sides—the strongest, most stable shape.

floor plan a picture of a room or series of rooms making up a building; a map of a building or room.

geometric shape one of a large number of visual shapes based on the principles of geometry.

geometrically stable shapes that can stand loading without changing shape.

hardline making sketch lines darker and more permanent.

hexahedron a six-sided, three-dimensional geometric shape.

icosahedron a three-dimensional geometric shape with 20 sides that are all equilateral triangles.

image a mental picture of an idea or object.

ionic the intermediate of the three classic Greek orders; columns distinguished by curved motifs resembling rams' horns.

key symbols, colors, numbers, etc. noted on a map or plan for the purpose of identifying important elements.

keystone the wedge-shaped piece at the top of an arch which holds the other pieces in place.

laminated beam a load-bearing member made up of many pieces glued or nailed together.

load the weight supported by a structure, wall, or beam

masonry construction with stone, brick, or concrete block, held together with cement mortar.

model a representation, usually in miniature, to show the construction or serve as a copy of something.

molding a decorative variety of shaped strips of wood or plaster used around doors, windows, ceilings, or roofs.

observations information or records obtained by watching, noticing, perceiving.

octahedron an eight-sided, three-dimensional geometric shape.

open space an area that invites you in.

order any one of the typical variations of the arrangements of columns, bases, capitals, and beams based on Greek architecture.

pace a measurement of length equaling a long but comfortable step.

paneled covered with wood or other materials made into sections to cover parts of a wall.

pattern a decorative design developed by planning, or the design observed in natural or man-made elements.

pediment a triangular shape at the end of a pitched roof over a series of columns.

plan a drawing made to scale to represent a top view or a view cut through a structure.

planning designing the arrangement of a building, or group of buildings, or a neighborhood, town, or city.

polyhedra many-sided shapes. If all sides are the same size, they are called "regular": if the sides are not the same size, they are called "irregular."

portico a porch that has a roof supported by columns.

post a vertical support such as a column.

preservation keeping up or preventing destruction of a building or area that is considered of historic or aesthetic value.

process a series of progressive steps for developing a project, considering alternatives, and producing solutions.

porportions the comparative relation between things as to size, width, length, height, and volume.

pyramid a shape with three triangular sides and a square base (may have a polygonal base).

record to report or list; a collection of observations, actions, or ideas.

rectangle a shape with pairs of unequal sides and all right angles.

reinforcement using beams, posts, braces, steel bars, or walls to make a structure stronger.

relief projection of parts of a drawing, painting, sculpture, or model.

remodel to reconstruct or make over.

repetition repeating a design motif or architectural feature to create an overall design.

resources the supplies and materials available from which to develop a design or structure.

rhythm a relation and interdependence of parts designed to become a harmonious whole.

roof pitch the angle of the slope of a roof.

rubbing laying a soft paper over a sculptured surface and reproducing its design by rubbing a crayon or pencil over it.

rural of the country as compared to being of a town or city.

safety factor a design element that makes a structure stronger than the figures show it needs to be so it will be sure to stand up.

scale the proportion of a drawing or model in relation to the actual size of the object.

sensory awareness to be aware of the sight, sound, smell, touch, or taste of an object or place.

single family a separate residence for one family.

shaft the central body of a column.

sketch to make a drawing simply or quickly.

space the three-dimensional volume of a room or area.

space bubble an imaginary series of spaces that surround people and within which various predictable kinds of activities happen.

span the space between two supports.

spatial relationships relation of spaces to one another or people to the spaces.

structure something that is built or constructed.

structural failure the breaking or bending of a structure because it is over-loaded.

structural member one of the supports of a structure.

suburban the area beyond the edge of a town or city.

support to hold up a load without giving way, or a part of a structure that does this.

survey to inspect, examine, and record information about a building, an area, or the activities of people.

symbol something used to represent or stand for something else.

symmetrical referring to parts that are the same on either side of a central line.

system a combination of things or parts that form a whole.

tension the stretching or straining of a structural member caused by applying a load.

tetrahedron a shape made up of four equilateral triangles.

texture the structure of the surface of a building, a material, or a work of art.

truss a combination of beams and other supports arranged in a triangle or collection of triangles to form a rigid framework to carry a heavy load and/or to span a long distance.

urban the area of a town or city.

variation different ways to create a solution.

visual communication the use of pictures, maps, plans, or perspective drawings to explain an idea, proposal, or design.

visualizing forming an image or picture in the mind or imagination.

warp the twisting or bending of a structural member due to the stress of loading.

Photo Acknowledgments

Jeff Albertson/Stock, Boston: 71 left
(c) Barbara Alper/Stock, Boston: 35 right
(c) 1981 John Blaustein/Woodfin Camp & Associates: 71 right
Fred Bodin/Stock, Boston: 141
(c) 1982 Timothy Eagan/Woodfin Camp & Associates: 34 right
Bob Ely/Stock, Boston: 35 left
(c) Elliott Erwitt/Magnum Photos: 61, 62
(c) 1982 Linda Ferrer/Woodfin Camp & Associates: 132
(c) Leonard Freed/Magnum Photos: 106
Clif Garboden/Stock, Boston: 15 center
Tyrone Hall/Stock, Boston: 137 left
Roy King: 145
Ira Kirschenbaum/Stock, Boston: 15 bottom
Norm Landes: 67, 139 right
Herbert Lanks, Black Star: 60
(c) 1965 Sergio Larrain/Magnum Photos: 13 top
Wayland Lee*/Addison-Wesley Publishing Company:
      135, 136, 139 left
(c) Danny Lyon/Magnum Photos: 34 left
Mike Mazzaschi/Stock, Boston: 66, 137 right
Peter Menzel/Stock, Boston: 15 top
Tom Stack/Tom Stack & Associates: 13 bottom

*Photographs provided expressly for the publisher.